BOLD
THE BIRTH OF FINE ART

MBUTA - LUYINDULADIO - CELLY

TATE PUBLISHING
AND ENTERPRISES, LLC

Published by Tate Publishing & Enterprises, LLC
127 E. Trade Center Terrace | Mustang, Oklahoma 73064 USA
1.888.361.9473 | www.tatepublishing.com

Tate Publishing is committed to excellence in the publishing industry. The company reflects the philosophy established by the founders, based on Psalm 68:11,
"The Lord gave the word and great was the company of those who published it."

Book design copyright © 2016 by Tate Publishing, LLC. All rights reserved.
Cover design by Dante Rey Redido
Interior design by Jake Muelle

Published in the United States of America

ISBN: 978-1-68319-824-6
Poetry / African
16.04.28

Acknowledgment

I only have the utmost reverence for the Queen, my dear mama, Luyinduladio Mponi, for your valuable teachings, care, blessing, and love. Gratitude is expressed to my father.

Contents

Preface

Where to begin and how? Not lost. Just thinking. The intent of *Bold: The Birth of Fine Art* is creativity, critical thinking, liberty, the exploration of the abstract, the absurdities of existence ought to be captured and expressed in this line of human experience and existence. I have been inspired by many. My intent is to carry the same torch and inspire few. Grateful, I am.

Respectfully,
Mbuta Luyinduladio Celly

A Maestro

Are you Wolfgang Amadeus Mozart?

No, I am not!

Are you Ludwig Van Beethoven?

Of course not! How can I be?

Then who are you?

I am the maestro without the orchestra.

I am the maestro floating in infinity.

I am Sir Montesquieu (full name, Sir Charles-Louis De Secondat, Baron de La Brède et de Montesquieu). Also, I am Dr. Frantz Omar Fanon, author of *The Wretched of the Earth*. Without a pen, extraordinary things are created and left in my mind only, so humans will not have the pleasure and privilege to enjoy them because they are unworthy of such honor and privilege until they stop killing each other. I guess they won't, and that is my only measure of their sanity. Outrage and critical, they will be with or without merit, mostly without merit. Still, I am the maestro without the orchestra. Always has been prior to birth, during birth, even after birth, the maestro of maestros or Maestri.

There Is Nothing

There is nothing of significance around except death.
    There is no tear to shed.
    There is no one to lie to except your own shadow.
    All have departed, and reality must sink.

Not Here to Please

I am not here to please, rather to offend, so your mind and
spirit can adjust accordingly.

I Am Offering

I am offering them the following with grace for their
enjoyment and savor. Tyranny! How can they decline? For
what reason and argument? Did they forget my title? King!
Majesty! Damn it! Heaven and hell be damned only if they
refuse or coercion will be used. As a result, they will have
to pray to God and evil for salvation. Let the guillotine be
ready! The king orders.

Liberty, Reason, Imagination, and Critical Thinking

Liberty, reason, imagination, and critical thinking—I am going to show you what they are, what they mean, and what they are meant to be. Please observe and learn attentively.

Lost Not Found

They think with some magical and nonmagical tricks they can lose everybody else. However, only some will be lost and not found. They simply don't possess the ability or the magic power to lose all else. Don't trust me on this if so wished.

Weight

How much weight do your true intentions carry?
How much weight do your lies carry?
How much weight do your words carry?
I'd like to know.

Explosion

Are you scared of the explosion? The explosion of great ideas, does knowledge scare you? Don't you want to liberate your damned mind from those irrational teachings and lies?

Power

Do you want power at all cost or not? Then we will acquire it the Machiavelli way.

What do you mean the Machiavelli's way?

Here's the book, *The Prince* by Niccólo Machiavelli, and do not only read but rather study it, and you would understand the journey we are about to embark on. It is called fate, the meeting with God, the meeting with the spirit of darkness, sinners, and death.

The Pitfall of Morality and Its Many Benefits

The pitfall of morality lies in murder, false accusations, lies, many enemies, betrayal, and so on. However, its many benefits are laid in truthfulness, courage, and the understanding of mankind. It is simply a matter of conviction; as you can see, the equation is not complex but extremely difficult to implement since sinners are at the center of all things seen and unseen.

Equally Dangerous If Not More So

They are showing me their respective armies to impress and make me fret. However, in the deepest silence possible, I say, I am equally dangerous if not more so with a pen due to the fact that great and genius ideas don't ever die but instead live on for eternity. These bastards do not get it even if explained day and night, so I speak in silence only. I am a dangerous man if not more so with nothing else but a pen.

The World and Its Many Problems

The world and its many problems—is this pure coincidence?

The racists and their disgraceful hate, where did they learn this disgraceful hate from anyway? When did they learn this disgraceful hate anyway? Who are they? What is their color? How does their darn mind work? Who blessed them with this obscurantic ability or mind-set? Pity! What a disgrace of grandiose waste!

I simply pity racist minds for their overwhelming ignorance and the spirit of obscurantism they carry within their minds and hearts. What a waste! What a disgrace! What a waste of human mind and heart! Make the spirit of darkness smile and be proud of you, bastards! Irony! Let their twisted minds imagine things of twisted nature. What else can be said? Pity! Only pity! And only pity is left, nothing else.

My Words

My words are not trickiest than any gospel, just truthful, authentic, and original. The universe will continuously ponder rightfully so.

Let Morality and Liberty Collide

Please let morality and liberty collide in full force. The final result is ugly and simultaneously beautiful. What a mess! A genuine mess built for the present and posterity.

Black Board Erased and Reinvented

He was as powerful as mankind can be, and he was and he is Black and will always be. The Black board erased and reinvented with forgery and treachery. When he spoke, the earth trembled, the volcanoes rose one by one; hell knelt and was set on fire. Oh! Heaven! Heaven prayed for mercy, and God was powerless to the power of the Black board. Black board erased and reinvented. So let the earth, hell, heaven, the mystic, and all sinners feel the power of the Black board. Black board erased and reinvented. The original beat, indefinable Black soul, power have been erased and reinvented countless times. Can they understand? Are you afraid of knowledge? Should you be? Black board erased and reinvented with a renegade mind. Renegade to the last breath, I am and intend to be. Damn Black fists in the air! Negus!

Lost Its Meaning Anyway

Lost its meaning anyway and go figure. Yeah! Fake as hell!

Energy, Power, Knowledge, and Death

I wish I could, but I can't. I do intend to leave the most
meaningful knowledge to mankind but not everything.
Energy, power, knowledge—the rest will be taken to my
grave without any regret, and not even the army of this
wicked universe can change this, and nothing is personal
just fate as it must unfold.

Can You Speak Your Mind Freely
So You Can Die a Free Man?

Can you speak your mind freely about God, the devil, the
corrupt governments, the corrupt religion, and damned
sinners so you can die free as a man? You must know the
answer. Watch me! Learn from the very best! Even though
these damned sinners are blessed with extraordinary gifts
from God, they are still damned. Who damned them? Is
God the author? Or is the devil the author? I deeply ponder.

Knowledge or Ignorance

Does knowledge scare you? Does ignorance please you? Does misinformation make you content? Does the world make you smile in its poverty, suffering, and death? Do you question God? Do you question the spirit of darkness? I insist. Do you question the force of obscurantism? Do you question religion? What excites your mind, knowledge or ignorance? Can you ignore knowledge? Of course, you can and die an imbecile.

The Taste of Greatness

The taste of greatness is defined and expressed in one word only. Legacy! How would you define yours?

Art

Always remember, people do not have to agree with whatever you create, but they must feel it. Make them feel the art, and that is the meaning of originality.

Check Me Out!

This is my unique order. Do not check me out, rather study me due to the fact that I am worth more than your imagination can reach or picture. I live in the millennia. Trust me on this.

Shaped by Destiny

Shaped by destiny, nothing is surprising to me, just others.

Stupidity

Why should I give this kind of stupidity and irrationality any value? Others have the opportunity to value both if so deemed. My spirit moves in the galaxies. Can you see it? Can you keep up? Can you touch it? Can you feel it? And they lie constantly that we have never contributed anything of significance to mankind, to history. And the least I can say is, this statement is laughable, racist, ignorant, and filled with uncharacteristic wicked spirits and intents. Can you handle the truth? Why can't you handle the true nature of the truth? Can you? Should I waste my time to teach this mindless brain? Or should I waste any time on these racist minds? Nah! Not worth a damn penny! Greatness and truth shall be taught elsewhere and taken to another dimension. How many times are you going to erase the Black boards and paint them whites? How many times are you going to steal again and again from Black geniuses? Dumb and imbecile we are not but believed to be by lost souls. Multiple thieves are standing next to us and claim to look for thieves for arrest. Fascinating thieves indeed! Yeah! Fool your own conditioned and confined mind to incomprehensible degrees and watch the free fall.

When all things are going to fall apart, who are you going to see in a matter of extremely limited seconds? Are you going to see God? Are you going to see the force of darkness? Are you going to see death itself? Are you going to see your own shadow? Are you going to see the truth? Are you going to see light? Are you going to see the same lies? What and who are you going to see? Let us wait and see then.

The Politics of Darkness

The politics of darkness are being planned and executed in absolute darkness by those dark minds. Can you understand the politics of darkness in darkness by dark minds?

The Universe Is Just a Grand Theater

The universe is just a very grandiose theater. As a result, just play your role, be it comical, grandiose, mediocre, worthy, unworthy, or whatever else that might be. Some sinners are very far away from satisfaction unless all kinds of death, pain, suffering, pity, misery are brought into the theater. Fascinating theater indeed! Fascinating performances! Fascinating sinners! Fascinating beings! I must say. Who gifted and damned them simultaneously? Is it God? Is it the spirit of darkness?

Reason

First, speak the language of reason and see if they can comprehend. These crooks may surprise you by reasoning, and if they do not surprise you by reasoning then, speak to them the language of guns, death, fire, and hell. I bet they will reason or die, and these will be the only choices left. I repeat and emphasize reason or death, so let them choose their own fate.

The Medicine

Here is the medicine that will cure your ignorance and simultaneously your soul. However, considering that your mind bears free will, therefore, you can certainly take it or do the opposite based on your free will only.

The Battlefield

Let us start the battlefield of ideas first and hopefully they will understand; if not, we will move aggressively in the battlefield with guns, fire, deaths, liberation, so this wicked system shall fall by means of all righteous necessity. And here we stand like real men and women do. Keep your damn Black fist in the air!

Mentally Imprisoned, Physically Free

I find myself somewhere at the corner of the earth willing to speak my mind. However, some sinners tell and warm me that I shall not due to the fact that this place is a dictatorship or a fake democracy, a forgery. I raise my being with certain grandeur and declare passionately that in the name of all mankind, in the name of righteousness, the will to liberty; the will to speak his or her mind freely shall not be punished nor suppressed due to fear and irrationality. Thus, liberty is not for the very few to enjoy but for all. I cannot bear the tragic thought of silencing my mind. How can they? How dare they? This fight will be won by reason or by guns and fire, and we welcome the challenge.

The Mistake and the Mystic

One of the greatest mistakes is to believe and think that there is a God while there is none. Or to think and believe that there isn't one while there is. The core question is how come they are still selling God to make a profit? Whether he exists or not is beside the point. Can the mystic be solved? Hasn't the universe paid enough by blood, sacrifices, deaths, treachery, and money? How come those false prophets of hell are still charging? How come religion is still welcoming forgery instead of the truth? I thought for a second that he is priceless since he is not; henceforth, give us the final price so we can pay it straight cash and get out of this slavery mentality once for all. Will this relationship between masters and servers live on to infinity? Sadly and with pity, amazingly entertaining indeed! Insanely unbelievable but believed. Or how in hell are they going to collect their money? Damn it! Pass the big and small collection buckets to sinners, and the rest can rest in history. Fascinating indeed! The very least must be said to conclude this insane chapter.

Gratitude

A simple thank-you sometimes is enough to express gratitude. Nothing more, nothing less.

Where Are We Going?

Where are we going?

We are going to meet our fate.

Where are we going?

We have a meeting with our destiny. Don't have to believe. Sit back, and watch with admiration.

Underestimate and Overestimate

Here is your ultimate warning. Please do not underestimate us and overestimate yourself. Otherwise stated, do not underestimate our abilities and overvalue yours to your own peril. Trust me on this.

Death at the Door

We say equality or death. You choose and tell us so we can implement one or the other.

The Title

I see from afar that you are waving your title proudly. The only thing I am concerned with. Is it given or earned? Is it manufactured or earned? Let me make this clear to your damn mind: this title can be given by the king or queen, the king and the queen. It does not matter to me, not a bit. The king, the queen, the title—all are forgeries. Thus, they can all go to hell. I will always obey my conscience, not the king or the queen. Fuck the king and queen! Include the title as well. Can you feel and see liberty deep down from my conscience? King, my ass!

Way Too Radical

They came to me and say that "I am way too radical." Sometimes they say it from private settings, forgetting for a second that this radicalism is the result of their racism, the result of their injustices, the result of their insanity, the result of their sins, the result of their continued war against us. I say I am not radical. Do you want a proof? Was I born radical? This damn world did not leave any other choices except to become radical in my convictions. Can you comprehend this? Even God and the spirit of darkness shall feel this wherever they are, wherever they are hiding.

Reason Left Their Souls

Reason left their souls a long time ago, and I do not know exactly when. However, in case you have any doubt, please check for yourself and try to reason with them.

Truth and Lies

The truth makes them uncomfortable, and their lies make us uncomfortable. Moreover, they claim to be the teachers of morality. Incomprehensible! Unbelievable! Insanity! Amazing and entertaining sinners indeed! It will be best and perfectly suited if they could only entertain their own condemned, conditioned, and damned minds. Contrary to the case is highly unfortunate and unwelcoming. Can you self identify in the painted picture?

The Citizen, the State, and Its Tactics

The state contends that my words incite violence, division, revolution, and a great treat to the state's existence. I laughed at such notion because the state possesses all the means to lead by example; however, the state chose not to and engages endlessly in the multiple criminal activities including murder of its own citizens. I am too dumb to know and realize that my writing will cause a treat to the state's existence as I addressed the state's presiding judge. Finally, the state condemned me to death. What else did you expect? My last words before my demise are "I never created this mess." "We inherited it from God, the spirit of darkness, and the state—all manifested in sinners' damned minds. The presiding judge and the state can go to hell! Renegade to the last breath, I am and intend to be." *Les apparences sont trompeuses.* (Appearances are deceptive.)

Intelligence and Ignorance

Intelligence is for the enlightener to appreciate and ignorant mind to ignore at all cost by all means and reasons even whenever the benefits are clearly explained.

The King's Bed

I would like to make you my queen in a king's bed literally and figuratively. Anything else would you like to consider queen? I am the king. Please don't ever forget this simple fact. Listen to treachery if your heart so desires. I am the king, and I have not forgotten, nor will I.

Comforting Death before Death

A drastic shift has to happen spiritually, mentally, and within the soul before death to not fear death in any form, be it administered by the crooked government unjustly or by sinners because they think they can or by the force of obscurantism or even God. The individual, the soul, will undoubtedly reach that light, that enlightenment where the universe meets the mystic, where the galaxies and the mystic fall apart, where the mystical spirit transcends human flesh.

They Must Be Conditioned
to Think as a Unit

They must be conditioned to think as a unit but not for their own good instead for their own distraction and destruction. Consequently, we can still steal all things of importance that belong to them. Isn't this genius? You convince me otherwise.

Don't You See?

Don't you see?
    Blood? Black!
    Ancestors? Black!
    Spirit? Black!
    All things? Black!
    Pain? Black!
    Joy? Black!
    Moves? Black!
    Bones? Black!
    History? Black!
    Conscience? Black!
    Origin? The Kongo Kingdom; therefore, Black!
    Gods? Black!

Religion? Doesn't have one. If it were the case, then Black is the answer! Not Arabic or European. I repeat, Black! Didn't they sell us in Zanzibar and many other places as well, did they?

Consequently and with eloquence, don't fool yourself. Black, you are born and will remain so just be original and true to the natural law. Nothing is wrong even if society convinces you the contrary.

And they convince the fools with ease that brilliance is not Black, doesn't have a Black name, and has never been Black. Well, just believe if you want to; as aforementioned, this is church after all. Don't you know that this is not a mosque or a temple?

Black board erased and reinvented with a renegade mind.

Liberty in treachery!

Treachery in liberty!

We sing and dance. The song, the dance, and the joy of treachery in all liberty without shame and remorse are all paradise on earth. Of course, we can justify all these and argue about them as well, even be philosophical. What else do you want to hear even see?

Only Black fists are raised in the air in another spiritual dimension. Can you see them? Are you certain?

Time on Earth

While I am travelling in the galaxies, a spirit asks continuously, "What did you do on earth? How was your time on earth? How was your journey?"

My spirit response is, "I meditated, learned, studied, matured, and left them knowledge. Understanding it is another matter." Then both spirits reached an extraordinary state of tranquility with ease and satisfied they were.

Strange Indeed

Treachery does not scare them; only righteousness does. Strange indeed! Not so strange indeed!

Trouble Is in Heaven

Here in heaven, we have an uninvited guest named the force of obscurantism. Can we foresee major trouble? Meanwhile, God is silent. Is heaven in trouble? What about the earth?

Shake the Earth

It is imperative, and this is expressed in the imperative form as well. Shake that tree so truth can fall and everyone can see it. Shake this tree so those multiple lies can fall as well and all can see. The truth is being confused within lies not anymore; even the blind men, women, and children can see now. They'd better run for eternity.

Intellectually Dishonest and Morally Corrupt

Intellectually dishonest and morally corrupt, then the question is, should you expect sainthood in all seriousness?

Necessity

Necessity must be done in order to satisfy the soul and mind, out of necessity.

Die they must, out of necessity.

Live they must, out of necessity.

Some may live, and others may die out of necessity.

Sins

The sons of anarchy are listing my sins so they can justify my death. As I stand unshaken, I say with absolute composure that those numerous sins are not mine because they all belong to the force of obscurantism and God without exception. Mine are here with me; therefore, those ought to be refuted categorically and accordingly. Death will come anyway at any time, so here I am, death. Thus, manifest yourself.

Sweet Talk

Not known to be a politician. Therefore, I cannot sweet-talk you with bullshit. Trust me on that.

Territory

This is the territory of insanity, and I emphasize once again: this here is the territory of insanity. Therefore, don't open it; don't cross it in any circumstances because you will open the gate of hell for eternity. Sinners continue to disobey and challenge the prohibition.

Value

As if reason was dead meaning ceased to exist, they continue to value and only see irrationality. May their sins be forgiven. I honestly ponder where their spirits fool around and that may explain their foolishness.

A Wise Man

When a wise man speaks, a wise listener will listen calmly in silence without a word; and when a fool speaks, a wise man must depart in silence without a word. *Sagesse* (wisdom) at its very best!

The Game

With their audacity intact, they never even asked but expected me to play this silly and wicked game of the master and the slave in reality. My answer to them is that even in theater and cinema I can never be a slave. So how dare they? I guess their soul lives in hell for eternity.

The World We Live In

The world we live in is just a formidable façade of lies and terrible entertainment for the enjoyment of the rich. Not all of them of course! Isn't this obvious? Aren't they the authors of pity and suffering? Do you expect them to say yes?

All Things

It has not been said yet even though known. All things shall return to their natural state, death, all without any exception.

The Voice of Reason

We implore, may the righteous spirit always carry us during the darkest time.

We implore, may our darkest spirits and tendencies find light and enlightenment.

We implore, may we commit insignificant sins since we are sinners by default. Finally, we express our significant gratitude to God for the blessings, including our ancestors.

God, the Spirit of Darkness, and the Crook

As the new recruits approach the master crook, he proclaims with an authoritarian voice, "Now! Kneel, my fellow brothers and sisters, and I am going to bestow upon you the blessings trusted in me by the spirit of darkness since God refuses to bless us." *What else can I say?* asked my pondering spirit. Well, just let them die in darkness since this is their own will and making. Freedom at its worst state of mind as illustrated.

Insanity

Many people are fed up with this insanity. Therefore, they can no longer protest with prayers only; their damn minds can no longer bear this insanity. To the contrary, they are demanding loudly and clearly to see God in flesh and blood. Will they obtain the satisfaction of their demand? Only God knows, and religion does not even know.

Opinion

Should her opinion count? Of course not!

Let me ask again just in case you did not hear me correctly. Should her opinion count?

Absolutely not!

Can you explain please?

Her opinion or opinions shall not count due to the fact that she is a bitch. A real bitch! Why would you commit the sin of valuing her opinion? To the contrary, I value women's opinions.

Suddenly, a girl asked me gently if her opinion counts. I said, "Yes, dear, it does." We both then just smiled and left the scene because we knew who she really was, a great woman.

Misery

I am looking at the Black's misery first. Then I looked at mankind's misery with the same consideration. Consequently, I came to the final conclusion that I cannot be anybody else other than the truest renegade. You can count me among the privileged if so deemed. Nonetheless, this status matters less as long as fellow humans are victimized, even killed, as a result of corruption mainly by corrupt politicians and irrational religions. Please save yourself, your own soul, then seek sainthood then saint yourself. Doesn't this sound good to your ears? In case it does not, then damn yourself. If your role is to save me, as a result, who is going to save you? Aren't you a sinner just like everybody else without any exception? I demand to see God himself in flesh and blood. Why not? Doesn't he exist? Theater and cinema, I have seen enough. Are you going to kill me for speaking my mind? Are you simply a murderer? Is this business as usual? We all have different purpose on this planet, I confess sadly and gladly. I come from the unknown, the galaxies, and the mysticism. Please be aware and do not dare to touch me.

You have been given life. Therefore, use it to impact mankind in the most positive way possible. By the way, don't take my advice and die as the greatest sinner of all or among the greatest. May the power of the righteous come and always be within us. Truest to the principles, renegade to the last breath.

Old Battles

Those old battles have been fought fiercely and won with a lot of prides and blood sacrifices. I heard some insane minds desire to go back. Well, they are allowed to dream just dream about those old good days as their characterize them. Sinners! You certainly can expect all things from them and dark spirits. Sinners!

Impostors

Please don't mind them because they indeed are impostors, great sinners, and fraudulent beings. Their crimes and lies are well-known. Their actions confirm that they have been damned since birth, probably prior to birth. Yeah! They can go to hell!

Pardon

Maybe they were born insane, and if this turns out to be true, they indeed have my pardon. Can any sinner explain? Or do we have to seek God's help? Can the spirit of darkness explain? Who else can? Thus, make your presence known. Should I beg?

Pensée Du Jour

I don't feel pity for myself. Thus, why should I feel it for others? They can feel it for themselves, can't they?

Freedom

Please go and tell Americans that they cannot have their freedom to bear arms, to free speech, to move as freely as the air, to think freely, and so on. Well, they will simply damn you, curse you, and kick you out rightfully so just ask England. Yeah! Those Brits! Or simply learn a little bit of history to find out. Damn right! This is America, not like any place else. I gladly refrain from cursing voluntary. Nonetheless, Americans get the point. Well, in case you don't, you will learn later. When did you get here?

Legendary

As the legend goes, he was the last man to fight tyranny. As the legend goes and grows, he was the last man to pay tribute to our forebears and God. A man of principle and morality as the legend always concludes. May our ancestors and God always guide us to the known and the unknown.

Folly and Only Folly

Yeah! Those Africans. Yeah! Those African bastards! Yeah! Those Africans who are always ready to sell their soul to the spirit of darkness for power, to have access to power, or to rule for eternity. Did they forget that death is inevitable? Yeah! Those African bastards who will do anything and everything for their masters so many Africans can die and suffer. Yeah! Those African bastards! Where's justice? Where is our due process? Justice cannot be found anywhere. At least we will find comfort or some type of justice with their deaths. Independence became a farce. Independence became dependence as ever seen before, just puppets running around in ridicule and disgrace, forgetting that many beings were killed to stop the ridicule. Comical! This is comedy! This is theater! This is cinema! This is parody! Where is God? The spirit of darkness is everywhere. Death, pity, folly, immorality, irrationality, and ignorance are all everywhere in this continent caused only by those damned African bastards and their masters. Yeah! Those African bastards! Folly and only folly! This is my assessment! Afraid of what?

Damn Black fists in the air! I am reporting to the ancestors, heaven, and hell. This is a new generation of Africans, not damned Africans. We are the Negus! We want all Africans' names restored throughout the continent. Damn

Black fists are floating in the air in another dimension. Can you see them? Are you sure? Are you certain? Keep your damn Black fists floating in the air! We stand proudly as Black Africans, as Negus! We have given this damn world our Black blood countless times. What else the heck do they want? They can never have our soul. Where is God? I dare to ask. Can you see us? Feel this if you can!

The Universe

This world is not a grandiose church, mosque, temple, synagogue, the assembly of corrupt politicians, or whatever else is out there meaning whenever they lie, and cause innocent deaths everybody has to fall in line without any questioning and just say amen. Of course, everybody won't fall for this theater. Needless to say that critical thinking has its great, and grandiose value including merit. Well, just sinners being at their worst state of mind and action. Only pity is left nothing else. Damn sinners!

The Kongo Kingdom

I carry within, in my blood, in my mind, in my soul, in my spirit, the Kongo Kingdom's mystic. Do I have to explain further? Nah! They won't comprehend. Thus, why talk to deaf beings? Why pain myself to death? I am simply Mbuta Luyinduladio Celly.

Kingdom

This is not a corrupt kingdom. As a matter of fact, this is not even a kingdom. Thus, you are not entitled to anything by birth. Go earn your own place by sweat and pain or be foolish in this universe. The very best is wished.

Sinners

Sinners are confused, and they think that I am around to save them in a religious sense, but clearly I am not. Why don't they figure out their own gigantic mess and remedy the wrongdoings?

Loyalty

All they offer is disloyalty, but they want my loyalty in return. Well, why don't they go to hell and damn themselves before I send them all there and damn them? Damn sinners!

Futile Noise

I dare to say that you are indeed just making futile great noise. Consequently, it is being evaporated in the air immediately. Ponder why?

Fascinated

Are you fascinated, aren't you? You tell me. How possibly could you not be? Can your mind seize the genius aspect of great things, things of divine nature?

Believe

A lot has been written and none of it is true but many believe and they have a right to believe not to threaten me.

The Divine

Can they touch the spirit of the divine? Nah! They can't, but they are allowed to dream, just dream, and lie.

Impostors! Vultures! I concur trick me again. Wait! How long have you been tricking us again and again? Is it possible that you can strike yourself out?

Farces

Do you really want to know the greatest farces engineered by mankind? Well, they are indeed in front of you, in your blood, in the way you think, in the way you conduct yourself, and they even evaded your traditions a very long time ago. Well, there are religion and politicking. In someway, they do some good to hide the farce, the buffoonery, and their own sins. Why don't you ponder how deeply there are so intertwined? Why don't you wonder about their similarities in character? They both create war, desperation, hate, and instability among mankind and nations. They are both unworthy of my reverence. Very few in this engineered farces are worthy since their respective implementations, and you certainly can count them with your fingers. However, they fill the history books with the highest praise possible.

What a farce!

What a shame!

What a dilemma!

What a pity!

What a scam!

What a sham!

Ah, sinners! What else can I really say?

The Call

Should I call upon my ancestors? Should I call upon the divine? Should I call upon the mystic of the Kingdom of Kongo? Should I call upon the very first Black ancestors who walked on this planet? To all dear beings, open the gate of knowledge, the past, the present, and the future. I ask with great reverence and gratitude. Please!

Blessed

I was blessed prior to my birth with unimaginable gifts; I mean out of the norm. Then I was blessed again during my birth and after my birth. Now! How are you going to bless me? Clearly, I don't need any blessing from anyone. Unique by birth, unique prior to birth, and unique after birth, I am.

Forgiveness or Revenge

Sometimes forgiveness is the only path left in order to purify the mind. However, sometimes revenge is the only path that can and must satisfy the soul and spirit. Please commit one or the other as you certainly see fit for your pleasure or displeasure. Good luck is wished. Needless to say you may need it.

Character

He looks dumb and acts dumb. Nonetheless, he is too far away from being dumb and stupid due to the fact that he plays a character to perfection. He is the most talented actor I have ever witnessed perform, theater at its very best, and buy it in case you so desire.

How Do You Create Extraordinary Art?

How do you create extraordinary art?

Well, you look at society. Well, you look and stare at destiny countless times. You spend countless hours pondering deeply in a spiritual journey only one person knows its significance, and that person is the author. You emerge and walk in spiritual darkness. Exponentially, you emerge, walk, float, soar, and shine in spiritual enlightenment. Endlessly, that is the beauty of being an extraordinary being with something significant and grandiose to leave to mankind.

Her Damned Shadow

Her damned shadow lives in the most wasted part of my brain simply due to the fact that she is a bitch devoted to debauchery, as well as a deep reminder of past, present, and future bitches. I currently ponder, does she know that you don't and can't fuck with me ever, bitch? How come she can't grasp this? Is she still stupid and a real bitch? I can guarantee that she is and will always be due to the fact that this state of affair runs in the cold blood. Reality can be sometimes dramatic, so let's reflect on that as well. Americanized is a matter of fact simply meaning I am and proud to be. Genius at the very best bitch! Should I throw a dollar bill in the air, bitch? Nah! You know what it means bitch, don't you? Or are you just too dumb? Yeah! I say with great confidence and swagger fuck morality. Yeah! Fuck it!

An Absolute Different
School of Thoughts

Are you blind or simply ignorant? Can't you see the obvious? Henceforth, let me state it for your senses, blind mind, and eyes. This is an absolute different school of thought. This is a revolutionary generation. This is a revolutionary blessed mind. The deep mystic is in the making of divine fate, things, and thoughts. This is not a show. However, in case your damn mind considers this to be, then enjoy the show.

Trust Me on This

As long as mankind's soul is imperfect, filled with greed, devil thoughts, calumny, and so on, the fight for righteousness will never cease nor ease. Trust me on this. We will profoundly continue to ponder incessantly the whereabouts of God and the spirit of darkness. Trust me on this. Please get me out of this damn theater. I have seen enough. Trust me on this. Finally, I don't fear my demise, and trust me on this because I say so firmly and with the deepest conviction possible. However, do not believe if so deemed. Aren't you a free man? Don't trust me on this.

Art

What is art? Art is simply the expression of expressing deep and hidden emotions, feelings including a certain vision, grandiose or mediocre, worthy or unworthy.

Life Is Just a Game

I am told that life is just a game. De facto, God and the spirit of darkness are the ultimate judges. I say with a golden silence, let us play this game and let them be the ultimate judges. My only hope is that both are going to be righteous, and if that is not the case, well, they can both go to hell. Let me chill in peace, would you?

Nothing to Prove

My spirit is sitting quietly in a golden and mystic silence at an undisclosed location, staring at death, and death is looking back at me. There is nothing else to fear or prove because I am supposed to travel this road anyway.

The Author of Many Sins

You are the author of many sins, and all of them can be forgiven except one. How and why did you dare to commit that unforgivable sin? You dare and have the courage to walk around me with the devil mask thinking in your damned being and spirit that I could never see nor find out. Wicked spirit can burn to hell for the ages. I only looked with pity and sadness and spoke only in my golden silence. Ooh, hell! Ooh, pity! What else is there to say? Nothing really.

I Could Have...

I could have explained, but they could not understand. I could have explained what I saw; however, they could have called me crazy and delusional within their limited minds and spirits. I could have told them specifically wherever I went spiritually, emotionally, in terms of vision. Nonetheless, I know with certainty that they could not comprehend due to the fact that these are things of another dimension open just to the very few. Thus, I do understand their incapability to grasp. As a result, I spoke only with a golden and mystical silence, and they cannot be blamed because this is just the nature of things in their natural order.

Dare to Dream

In your pain, I say, "Dare to dream."
    In your trouble, dare to dream.
    In your suffering, dare to dream.

In your glory, be kind, and I emphasize, dare to dream because nobody should tell you otherwise.

If the world ever dare to oppress you, dare to dream and fight back with all your strength.

Noble Blood

This thing does not deserve my noble blood, not even a drop. Others can have it, and I do not intend to look back. In case I ever do, this will be done with amusement and sarcasm only.

Knowledge

It is easiest to speak with ignorance and lies rather than knowledge and truthfulness, and that is the truest nature of mankind.

The System

He is the head of a corrupt system that protects him in many ways. Thus, don't expect change, but dream it if you so wish, and this wish becomes true in some way. Yeah! That's all there is to say. Good luck, dreamers!

The State and the System

You must be glad that the state and the system do not manage our thoughts and both do not understand its origin. Otherwise, many of us will be thanked by death and death only, if not all of us for opposing the state and the system, for exposing the farce, the façade, the corruption, even just for speaking our righteous mind in a society that is supposed to be representative of its citizens. God probably knew so we can certainly call him the Incomprehensible Genius. What happened to all the righteous promises by the state and the system? What happened to liberty? How come liberty became treachery? Never underestimate our righteous will to fight back, and this is the closing argument.

Playing Chess

What are you doing, sir?

I am playing chess.

Well, I don't see a chessboard or an electronic device being used.

Well, sir! I am playing in my mind, literary and figuratively in a simultaneous manner.

Well, sir! Who is the opponent, or who are the opponents?

Well, sir! This will be best if left questionable, and with all due respect, please give me a second. I need to close my eyes for few seconds.

Very few could understand, but he could.

Well, sir! The pleasure is always mine, and you will be best left alone since this is destiny. Extraordinary is the only thing left to say rightfully so.

Logic

I am sorry to say, but he does not comprehend logic in its outmost mathematical basic form. Thus, I recommend that you start with arithmetic before moving to math because both arithmetic and math have their rationality, and you must have a sense of logic in order to grasp, so ask God to give him some sense of logic. In case He refuses since He possesses the liberty to do so, then command the devil to get out of his mind and life. Only and only then we shall proceed to the teaching.

The Wizard of Absurdity and Illusion

The wizard of absurdity and illusion is here among us, and we ask secretly to all to listen to all things he says. However, proceed in doing the opposite.

Thanked Faithfully

Now they are thanking faithfully the oppressor for oppressing them. Please don't try to comprehend because their souls are at another place filled with confusion. Fascinating sinners! I just ponder, was this part of the plan at the origin of the oppression? Or did the oppressor figure this out when the oppression was in full mode and strength? Extraordinary indeed!

The Rise and Fall of the Establishment

The rise and fall of the establishment are well-established just read history. The French Revolution in 1789 is a fitting example. The fall and rise of the establishment always fall and rise with corruption including many other factors tied to corruption. Bastards always want power to rule all else. Yeah! Those bastards! They don't seem to learn anything else except corruption. Fascinating beings! Who did send them on earth anyway? I ponder.

By Reason or by the Language of Death

Eh! You! Suckers! Yeah! You! Damned sinners! This conflict you invented against me by wicked spirits and means. How do you want to solve this, by reason or by the language of multiple deaths spoken only by guns and fire?

Legendary Blood

Please tell me what kind of blood run in your veins?

You really don't want to know, do you?

Of course, I insist.

Well, my spirit, my body, *ma raison d'être*, and my veins run the noble blood of the Kongo Kingdom, the legendary blood of renegades, the blood of legendary warriors, the combined blood of African renegades, the legendary blood of geniuses, the legendary blood of visionaries. And that is the simplest answer. This is a tribute to all my forebears in their own grandeur and weakness. The next generation must know that we never came up from trees as the lie is to be said over and over again, or as the lie is recounted countless times so call this the tree of genealogy. Arc you satisfied? There is nothing else to say.

Yes, I am.

The Change Claimer

Even the change claimer played with the system, within the limits of the system, then got outplayed by the system.

Were his intentions noble?

Nah! The change claimer is just a very skilled salesman with the aim to deceive also a puppet of sort. I mean an extraordinary and gifted con artist. Sad to say, but I don't even have any hope left. What a sad end! The only remaining comfort I have left is the theater is at the end, but the discomfort is, the theater continues. This may seem complex to certain minds. Nonetheless, it is not because your brain can definitely figure out this nonmathematical complex equation. I assure you.

Misery!

Eh! Look at misery! She is staring at you. Do you want to grab it, pick it up, clean it, or continue your path with happiness? Misery!

Revenge

They say revenge is sweet. I say mine is bitter and cold like a medicine. A medicine that has only one purpose: to kill, not cure.

Not for Sensible Minds

This is not for sensible minds because God is questioned in length, the spirit of darkness is shown the gates of hell, and sinners are dissected from different angles. This state of creativity was meant to be, and fate is unfolding as it must.

Luck

I asked God if I had any luck left. He said no. I asked the spirit of darkness, why did he steal the rest away? He did not answer, so I said, "Fuck you! I can create my own luck."

Truth, Theater, and Cinema

I told you the truth persistently. Nonetheless, you refuse to believe continuously. Consequently, I switched the matter to theater and cinema, and you believe with a great smile.

Henceforth, I logically conclude that you love theater and cinema to death, so you will have both until death. Are fools born or made of to be? I ponder.

Lost Soul

Even God cannot and will not save them. Now do you understand that death is their sole destiny plain and simple? This can be strange to others, not me, so let them meet their destiny, death.

Not Many Just One Reason

Please give me one reason why they should live, and I will give you a trillion why they shall die, die immediately without delay of any sort.

Offended

Offended, they claim to be concerning everything I say or write, and offended I claim to be for their lack of honesty, for their actions, for their silence whenever deemed unnecessary, even their distorted speeches. Strange indeed as I find myself in this position, this place, I concluded.

How Do We Play This Game Called Life?

We play this game called life with murder, corruption, deceit, assassination, lies, and don't ever dare to think or conclude that prayers are going to save you—I mean, us. Thus, let us play them—I mean other beings—as we know best. Should I curse here or not? No need to. Your composure must be gold in this case. Keep it clean, and let's move and let those suckers feel us at our very best. At our very best, even God is going to reward us with paradise including countless prices and surprises. Does it get better than that? You convince God and report back to the earth—I mean, to all sinners? What kind of role do you want to play among all sinners? And here is my last word for you. Genius!

Heaven and Hell

I sincerely hope that heaven and hell exist; otherwise, we are spending countless hours wasted for nothing and rubbish, which we could have spent rightfully so doing some good for heaven or committing a lot crimes for hell. Don't we already do that? I guess so. Irony of ironies!

Punishment

What should their punishment be, sir?
Death!
Anything else should we consider, sir?
Nope!
The verdict has been clearly rendered and death it is unambiguously. Proceed with joy.

Dishonesty at Its Peak

Whenever stupidity reaches unfathomable degree of dishonesty and disgrace, you ought to laugh and turn your back on it forever. Otherwise, don't be stupid on your turn. What else can you really do? Do not contemplate death and murder, not worth the pain.

Check My Black Blood

Creativity runs profoundly in my blood, spirit, and mind. As a result, I have nothing to prove just check my Black blood.

Free Will

Why would you want to amplify your misery to great length willingly? I guess free will can play to our own disadvantage sometimes however still worth having.

Fundamental Real Change

I say loudly and clearly that everything must change fundamentally, not some but everything. Yeah! Go figure! Don't you have a brain?

Noise Everywhere

Wherever I look, there is noise; and wherever I don't look, there is still noise.

In someway, somehow, religion wants to control my being and life.

In someway, somehow, the spirit of darkness wants to control my life and mental state.

In someway, somehow, society, which is full of rubbish, wants nothing else except to control my being, state of mind, and my movements according to its irrational traditions.

Finally, I am told that God created us free; nonetheless, I ought to obey God with fear and submission.

Well, well! I am looking inside my being, mental state, and soul, only one question emerges. Can't I be absolutely free without any friction?

With certainty, I know the answer to this question unquestionably. Not confused at all.

Stuck in the System

How worst are you stuck in the system? I recommend that you beat it with honesty if and only if you can. I mean if you have the mental strength and capacity. And in case you can't, please beat it with dishonesty because others do. The question is, why not? Nothing matters, and this is real life, not some utopia or bad dreams. The last words belong to you. This is your decision to make. Go ahead and choose. Good luck is wished, and I know you may need it.

Weep in Silence

They continuously say for erroneous reasons and motives that "we must always weep in silence." We, Black people, we, Africans, can never accommodate that demand or order, and the universe ought to know this. Well, simply put, the universe shall tremble every single time we rise.

Dissenting Voices

Is this a farce or a democracy?

How come there are no dissenting voices as if this is a perfect paradise or a perfect hell? Ooh! Shame on a sham!

Ooh! Sham without shame!

What a shame!

What a sham! Pity for the sham! Pity for the shame!

Let their damned minds rest in a certain state of mind so we can have peace and loot fearlessly.

Praying

They are praying for our death countless times, and implementing this, meanwhile we are praying for their resurrection. Strange indeed!

Not a Changed Man

Not a changed man offered us change and hope simultaneously.

What a sham!

What a fallacy!

Many bought the sham literally for what it was not, the truth. And the sham was sold at all different prices from the lowest to the highest, especially to crooks. Moreover, the crooks sold us the sham in return using a Black mask, a Black face. Don't believe and check the scam for yourself; believe your own eyes.

Insanely unbelievable! Why can't they make me king then? The makers of dreams and illusions are among us, making a mockery of our courage and fights.

Not Here Yet

Not here yet, but there will be a time when sorrow and catastrophe will come, will become a great deal.

Who will stand up?

Will you?

Will you sell your own kind to the spirit of obscurantism?

What is money without a spirit?

What is the value of existence with a dead soul, spirit, and mind?

Worthless!

And many minds will willingly choose worthless.

Never Forget

Have you forgotten?

Don't you remember?

Who cleaned your memories and history?

Who falsified them?

Treachery in liberty!

Liberty in treachery!

The teachers of morality have become and gone insane; the civilizer of all things, irrational and immoral.

Never forget in case your brain possesses this tendency of intellectual laziness or just the opposite of truth. I am a man, a Black man, an African Black man, a Black king, a Negus in Amharic, with all the credentials embedded within stretching back to the beginning of time, to the very first Black African ancestors, the truest kings and queens of all, the originator of all mankind, the originator of the rest. Our deepest reverence is being paid to the truest kings and queens of the origin.

Never Forget Again

Never forget again in case your brain possesses this tendency of intellectual laziness or just the opposite of truth. I am a queen, a Black queen, an African Black woman with all the credentials embedded within stretching back to the beginning of time. Meant to be by his side. Meant to be this way.

Insanity Does Not Reason

Insanity does not reason without force. I mean brutal force. Thus, you know what kind of remedy you must implement if deemed necessary.

A Mind without Knowledge

A mind without knowledge or falsehood is as dangerous as a weapon of mass destruction if ever activated to its fullest capacity of imbecility, stupidity, ignorance, tragedy, nonsense, and evil knows this.

God

These are not beliefs but facts for the believer.

Isn't God the creator of the universe? Yes, he is.

Isn't God the creator of all things? Yes, he is.

Isn't God then the creator of all things rational and irrational by implication?

Isn't God the creator of the force of obscurantism?

Isn't God the creator, the ruler of all things seen and unseen? Yes, he is.

Don't you love your liberty, but want to blame God for all ills?

Isn't he the creator? Yes, he is.

Isn't he the most powerful to a degree unknown to mankind? Yes, he is.

Isn't this just an irony of sort?

Confused, I am.

Amused, I am not.

Shocked, they are.

Shocked, I am not, so let them be!

From Darkness to Light

From darkness to light, light must shine on these darkest souls, and this is imperative.

I Could Have Forgiven If...

I could have forgiven and understood if they sold the revolution to God but to the opposition. Damn! How damned are we? How damned are they?

Damn!

If they had sold our bloody revolution to God, I could have forgiven and understood, but they sold it to evil. Damn! How damned are we? How damned are they?

Shadow of Death

He died in disgrace, and his shadow of death was still present and smelling pity, lies, and crimes. Difficult to fathom, isn't it?

War on Black People and Africa

If this endless war continues on Black people and Africa, then Black people and Africa must rise up and demolish this wicked challenge once for all. The earth, hell, heaven— all must tremble with the force of volcanoes so ultimate renaissance and liberation must happen.

Rise! Africa, rise!

Rise! Africans, rise!

Oh! Oh! Great ancestors, we invoke your wisdom and courage.

Being Tortured by Stupidity and Ignorance

I am being tortured by stupidity and ignorance literally. The only course of action I see is to leave in silence.

Please Tell Me

Please tell me uncomfortable truths as opposed to comfortable lies. If so pleased, you can definitely reserve those comfortable lies to those whom the mind excites. Thus, I am listening.

I Will Show You

I will treat you well and show you the gates of heaven if you show me kindness and love, and in the same manner I will show you the gates of hell if you dare to fuck with me. Take notes and leave me at peace, says the generous spirit.

This Is a Matter of Spirituality, Not Physicality

This is a matter of spirituality, not physicality. I smell death at the door. Please enter.

"Are you ready?" Death asked.

"Nope! I am not."

"Well, I am going to travel with you from now on to protect you against your enemies who wish death upon you. Henceforth, you only can depart when your time comes," Death explained.

Only a mystic silence was my response to the reality of death.

A Dangerous Man

The crooked state called me a dangerous man, and I retort that the crooked state is indeed the danger to mankind and liberty. Henceforth, revolution by all means so the state can learn how dangerous of a man I am.

Being Protected

While some are urging me to seek God's protection, others in the same manner are recommending the force of obscurantism.

I stayed silent and reached out to the galaxies, then replied that I don't need either because I am being protected by Death. Now let them ponder!

The Problem

What you fail to comprehend is, the problem is not to move the bodies first but minds; then the bodies will automatically follow the motion of the mind. Finally, the marching of revolutionary minds can commence and destroy immorality. Imperatively, do not dare to misunderstand this again to your own peril, including the peril of humanity.

In the Absence of Logic

In the absence of logic and reason, only guns can speak and may they rest peacefully in hell.

If I Were Asked...

If I were asked to choose between a European lie (God) and an Arabic one or whatever else is out there, I will always choose the African Black ancestors because the godly Black blood runs within to an unfathomable degree, and I cannot explain further.

This Was Thought to Be Impossible

They came to me and said, "This was thought to be impossible."

And my reply is, "This was thought to be impossible, just in your minds, including theirs, not mine." Now, conclude as you see fit.

Be It in Your Face Racism or Hidden

Be it in your face racism or hidden, I move to a spiritual space and place unreachable and unfathomable by the racists; in that space and place, things are holiest by nature.

The Aim

My aim is not to impress but defend myself against this tyrannical system called the government. You don't have to believe me; just look at its history, its countless murders, its crooks, its laws, its thirst for mankind's blood, its irrationality, its immorality, the murder of its own citizens, its stolen properties and land. Ironically, the government wants to teach something about liberty, decency, and democracy. Strange indeed for the victims! Not so strange indeed for the looters! Vive, anarchy! What a world!

Your Enemy, and Don't Become Your Worst Enemy

Whatever your enemy does, you must study, comprehend, and master.

If your enemy uses the concepts embedded in *The Prince* by Niccólo Machiavelli, then you must study these concepts or whatever else is or is not.

If your enemy claims one thing and the outcome is always another, you must figure out this trickery and master it to the best of your ability for your own benefit.

In case you are ignorant, lazy, stupid, and fail obviously to comprehend all these, consequently, don't be surprised by your demise because you are indeed your worst enemy, and that is the reality of this wicked world.

Life Is a Matter of Choice

Life is a matter of choice between evil and purity. Thus, in a state of conscience or conscienceless, you must always choose.

What You Fail To Understand

What you fail to understand is, the fact of the matter is, I am not like any man and any man is not like me either. In other words, I am unique by birth and spirit. I beg not to be tested.

Never Fail to Impress Me

Stupidity and imbecility never fail to impress me. Should I not be?

The Con Artists

The con artists are everywhere, claiming to be everything they are contrary to be.

They claim to be men of God.

They claim to be prophets.

They don't claim to be con artists, but they are.

They claim to be leaders of the masses.

They claim to be moral politicians.

They claim to be all things.

They claim to abide by the will of God.

All beings are not fools, just some.

Hell, since these beings speak and act for you, can't you just call all of them back home? Thus, we can have the peace of mind, and hell on earth can cease immediately.

Please Do not Worry about Me

Please do not worry about me because:

I have seen this and that in my dreams and reality.

I have walked into fire before the glory.

I have been into the galaxies.

I have seen death before death.

I have meditated long enough.

I have taken my place among the ancestors.

The earth is burning; you must worry about your soul.

Finally, my soul, spirit, and mind can rest peacefully because all have done what is possible.

Not Looking for Sympathy

Not looking for sympathy. We are looking for action, fairness, equality. Until then, please take your sympathy somewhere else.

Human History

If you read human history in its truest form or even its forged one, mankind's genius and barbarism are both apparent even to the blind. Thus, why do they forge history?

The Impossible

They insisted that "the impossible can not be done," and we completely agree except our vision was not and is not impossible. Case in point, just watch our genius at work, and let it speak for itself.

Perfection

Perfection is a work in progress, and nothing comes easy. No matter how challenging, we are still marching toward this ideal.

These Ideas

These ideas must triumph and stand on their own merit, not the contrary because they are righteous.

We don't need to use guns, fire, and death. Do we?

We Would Like These Ideas to Stand

We would like these ideas to triumph and stand on their own merit, but they can't unfortunately. Therefore, guns must speak the language of death so reason can return.

As I Critique

As I critique, they can, and they need not to be reminded nor worried. As I critique, they shall, because it is a birthright, as the point shall be emphasized since tyranny is near and being implemented elsewhere.

They Are Urging Me...

They are urging me to convince the insane. My response to this matter is it is impossible, and I leave you all the pleasure and benefits by trying. I should proceed to other matters of significant importance. Good luck is wished with all sincerity.

Worst Conclusion

They came to their own worst conclusion that I am the personification of hell according to their religious beliefs, and I concluded that they can keep believing that they are indeed the perfection of heaven even though it is contrary to many facts. Then I departed gladly with the rest of my many thoughts.

I Ponder

I ponder.
> What should satisfy them, democracy or tyranny?
> Should they experience both or just one?
> The answer is not obvious to me.
> Is this answer obvious to them?
> I ponder again.

Pay Back

First, you must understand these are the corrupters, crooks, and the authors of countless miseries. How should we pay them back with revenge or forgiveness? I ponder.

The Mind

The mind must impose its own silence and discipline in order to navigate things of holy and celestial nature. Only if deemed necessary, the universe must tremble.

Accused

Accused by the government for unproven highest treason in reciprocity, I accuse the government of proven multiple murders of its own citizens. Who shall die first of unnatural death? That is the question to be asked since the government concluded this is a matter of existence or demise.

Only Conditional

If this crooked government continuously implements injustice, inequality, murders of its own citizens, immorality, and what else, then the simple conclusion is it must have come from hell. Therefore, must be replaced immediately and unequivocally by the opposite.

Don't Question me

Don't question me question yourself because you may find this process rewarding and useful whether you cross the line of sanity or not.

Pointless

You cannot navigate these great ideas with them due to the simple fact that they are unworthy of the honor. If you dare, they will undoubtedly prove this to you.

We Don't Capitulate

The following must be clear in the mind of crooked governments. We don't capitulate in face of danger; we stand unapologetic for the masses and justice. The fight must go on even in the face of death and murder. Stand up! Rise up! We are going to, and here we are.

Malady

How long are we going to put up with this malady, the malady of the corrupters and racists? History must record my discontent in full mode. They don't scare me, never have and never will. Damn Black fists in the air, Negus! Do not test our will! I beg not to be tested.

They Screw the Country and the World Simultaneously

They screw the country and the world simultaneously and seem not to comprehend why the heck the country is mad. Why the heck the world is torn apart by wars, hunger, and anger? Those clueless politicians are bred differently from hell to say the least. Sometimes they want to silence us by the bullet and murder. They must be damned!

I Am the Captain

I am the captain of my own ship and can bestow the title General as well to my liking if deemed necessary. This simply means I do as I pleased. Can't you follow this example?

This Mess

This total mess has been here for centuries and millennia, and they expect this generation to fix this with magic. Aren't they among the authors, are they? Why should we listen to them anyway? Aren't the enormities of mistake apparent even to the blind? Shame without shame is characterized by shameless.

Do You Want to Enter?

Do you want to enter that spiritual space where things of celestial nature are not seen but deeply felt and are inexplicable to ordinary beings? Well, you have to be chosen by the spirit of righteousness, and I do not choose.

Justice Must Be Served

Justice must be served otherwise society must be burned not only with rhetoric but also literary. The consequences are not being invented; rather, they are well-known throughout history. Thus, choose to serve justice for all, as a wise man would advise.

Exercising Liberty

A spirit asks me the following:
Why do you think the way you do?
The answer is simple: I am exercising liberty.
I am exercising the principles of righteousness.
I am exercising objectivity and realism.
I am questioning things that deserve to be.
I am questioning the status quo as it must be done.

The Manuscript

The manuscript is being written; however, the audience would like to know the end of the final chapter. The answer is she dies.
Why does she die, and how?

She dies of her own multiple and various lies, so she trips on her own sword. Therefore, she dies of an amusing death while God and evil are both looking at her from nearby.

Couldn't she be saved?

The simple answer is no, due to the fact that her death is a factual testament that she could not be. However, the complex answer is that she could have been if and only if both God and evil were willing to save her or just God or may be just evil by stopping the trickery of her mind.

The audience is confused, so let it sync, but they applaud anyway as the curtain is being dropped.

Fascinating brilliance!

Simplicity

They are sadly unable to grasp simplicity.

How can they grasp complexity?

Are they doomed by nature or by their own damned mind?

Fascinating to watch and not amused.

Trick

How do you trick your own mind to falsify the simple truth and fact that cannot be? I would like to comprehend but can't unless we are in theater and cinema.

Evil, can you explain?
God, can you explain?
Who else can?
This irony must be evil.

Crying

While the masses are crying for justice and equality, the very few are crying for corruption and tyranny. I wondered for a second if I were living in hell literary. Then I saw them with a diversity of religious books convincing me literally that I was not living in hell. Simply put, this is hell on earth as I realized. Tears are falling incessantly; even the dead are crying. Only pity is expressed.

The System Is Tyrannical and Corrupt Anyway

The fact of the matter is the system is tyrannical and corrupt anyway. Can't we destroy it by reason? Should we prepare for war and revolution? These are not easy choices by nature, so think deeply well of the consequences before the commencement of the march, the march of liberation.

The Rule of Law

They love the sound of the rule of law without believing its meaning, and if and only if they believe its great meaning, then I know with profound conviction that I can express my discontent without any fear of tyranny. I do so without fear of tyranny of any government on earth. Let the rule of law rule all of us without discrimination or favoritism.

Aren't we in paradise?

I Am Simply Who I Am

I am writing these great and grandiose ideas while sick with a cold and fever. I think the moment is worth capturing. Inspiration at its very best is quite extraordinary, incomprehensible, and unstoppable. The desire to leave something of significant magnitude to mankind is a reason only destiny can explain, but destiny is mute even as I never cease to ponder.

There Is Something

There is something intrinsically genius and dark about the human spirit supported by numerous facts and opinions.

I Do Not Pretend to Be

I do not pretend to be an expert on this matter and subject. However, the only thing I can claim to know is that art must speak to the soul and spirit of mankind in order to be felt with emotions including a certain degree of appreciation.

Arrogant

After reading my writing, they came to conclusion that I am a great, arrogant man. I simply contested in silence then came to my own conclusion that I am indeed a quiet, arrogant, and defiant volcano, and they can ask God or the force of darkness for confirmation if so deemed necessary. Arrogant is indeed the correct adjective, and I take this characterization with both humility and arrogance. To conclude this chapter, only arrogance led me to greatness, compassion for mankind, including the thirst for knowledge. Thus, I accept your assessment without arrogance.

Life

Life will test your convictions and character. I hope that you are ready or in the process of being ready. Do not let the degree of darkness define you. This is not heaven; it is real life on earth with good and bad people—not theater, not cinema, I must emphasize.

Morality Has No Place Here

Morality has no place here, just immorality, and I must add that we have carte blanche from heaven.

What is the trick?

There is none, and if there is one, I am not aware of it as far as I am concerned. May your critical thinking be in motion here.

The Nation

The profound and fundamental character of this nation must change in the direction of righteousness that is the expectation coming out from the people. Don't sell your soul!

Who Are We?

Who are we?

Are we the lost generation or the sacrificed one?

Are we the generation that will eventually give a new meaning and direction to the world?

Should we be the hopeless generation?

How should we embark on this challenging journey called life?

Who are we, and where do we want to go?

How do we achieve harmony in a broken world?

How do we navigate these challenging matters?

I dare not to answer these questions.

Natural State

All opinions and feelings must be put to rest due to a simple known fact with respect to this matter that all living matters shall return to their natural state, death, all without any exception.

Please Learn

Please learn how to amuse yourself and others. Be a comedian. It may not be a fruitless career.

They Cannot Be Trusted

Their actions speak volume. Thus, they cannot be trusted if they believe I don't; and if they don't, then I do.

Calamity

They are challenging the human mind to respond to this calamity to say the least, and trust me it will because the human mind possesses a reservoir of creativity and greatness.

It Must Rhyme and Flow

It must rhyme and flow like the Black great blues and jazz.

It must rhyme and flow like the Congolese great rumba as illustrated by the great Luambo Makiadi, Tabu Ley, Tshamala Kabaselé, and many others.

It must rhyme and flow as composed and played by the revolutionary Bob Marley and the Wailers.

It must rhyme and flow as demonstrated by the great African griot.

It must rhyme and flow to the African beat, invention, greatness, and vision.

It must rhyme and flow to the African drums beat and tam-tam.

Simply let it flow and rhyme, and let the spirit carry us.

In your own liberty of many opinions and lies, convince yourself and others that genius is not African and has never been Black.

Soar, rhyme, and flow in the name and power of the African ancestors. Here we are. Here we stand as always in righteousness and defiant as never seen before.

Can You Escape?

Can you escape? If you do not see my grandeur in hell, you will see it in heaven.

Can you escape? If you do not see my grandeur on earth, you will see it in hell.

Can you escape? If you do not see my grandeur in heaven, you will see it in creation; as a matter of fact, just relax.

Spiritually, I call upon things and living matters of celestial and holy nature.

Imagine the Universe Without Us

Imagine the universe without us; there is and there will be nothing to see and touch.

Imagine the universe without us; there is only emptiness and nothingness.

Imagine the universe without us; there is no creativity and procreation.

Imagine the universe without us; there is no continuity.

Imagine the universe without us; it is simply unfathomable. Can you fathom this? Please entertain your own mind and spirit if you can. I tried at the very best to entertain mine, but I can't.

I Always Thought...

I always thought that I will wake up in heaven after my demise, but I woke up in hell. I wonder what happened.

I always thought that I will wake up in hell after my demise; instead woke up in heaven. I ponder what happened.

I always thought that I will wake up either in heaven or hell after my demise. However, there is no hell or heaven.

What a treachery!

What happened?

Can I get my money back? Is it too late?

They Minimize Our Impact

They minimize our impact on earth with treachery and lies, but we navigate the spiritual atmosphere and universe differently. That is all there is to know. The knowledge is concealed forever, and they can never access everything that belong to us, just us. They are allowed to dream, dream in fantasies and lies. Bon voyage! I must say.

My Intention Is to Build, Not Destroy

My intention is to build not destroy, and if this requires looking into darkness sometimes, let bravery and the lens of spirituality accompany me.

Marriage

If you are going to experience only hell in a marriage, why experience the headache? Just a reminder, there is another in line. However, if you are going to walk in this labyrinth of unpredictability and predictability with a little bit of pain and a lot of love to heal that pain, then this walk is worth the memories. A last thought of consideration, I am unfit to advise because experiences will teach and advise. My enduring hope is you find enduring love and happiness.

I Want Liberty

I want liberty.

Even in heaven and hell, there is no such thing as liberty. Thus, why would you want liberty anyway and to do what? The government asks.

Of course, the irony is the government can do as it pleases, commit countless murders, increase your taxes to death, create impunity for the haves, condemn the have-nots, kill its own citizens with the pretext of rubbish, and the list goes on to infinity.

Street of Darkness

I walk these streets of darkness with light in my mind, and Death never leaves me because it is here with certainty to protect me against all enemies, seen and unseen, and I feel sorry for all my enemies without further elaboration.

Timeless

Only time will judge if this creativity is timeless or not, and I hope it is and inspires.

Never Dare to Threaten Me

Never dare to threaten me because I will give you death as a present and send you to hell.

This Is Not Church

I am told to obey without questioning, and my reply is I am going to question without obeying. As far as I know, this is not church. Should the masterful character of my mind be put to rest and waste without questioning? The enormities of my doubts are relevant not irrelevant with respect to these matters.

Knowledge Has Never Been Free

The burden of ignorance must be lifted. Knowledge has never been free. To the contrary, it has always been paid with money, hard work, sweat, pain, and great discipline, be it mental or spiritual. Sometimes it has been even paid by blood and death unfortunately.

Mediocrity or Excellence

Why aspire to mediocrity when you can aspire to greatness and excellence?

Some Kind Of...

I am ignorant where he or she has gotten this kind of clumsiest and extraordinary conviction that I am some kind of Negro, but I am not, never is, never has been, never will be. I am the Negus. Check my Negus blood if you can't tell. It goes back, time and time again with absolute certainty to the Kongo Kingdom, and there is something mystical about it. How do you go from the kingdom to being a stolen property? I am certain someone can explain with treachery and liberty as accustom. Can't they? Heaven and hell, their masters, owe us a reasonable and satisfactory explanation if their existence is unquestionable since everywhere I look all I see are a combination of lies, lies, and layers of lies. And I am disturbed as reflected by the navigation of my soul and spirit. How could this be? How could this happen while a supreme guardian of righteousness exist? The absurdities of existence while we exist are unfathomable, maybe insolvable as well. What a trick! Where is the trick? Who is the author of the trick and treachery?

Disregard Those Damn Rules

Disregard those damn rules.

Then can't everybody just disregard those damn rules?

Of course not, just us not everybody. Are you stupid? This is not paradise.

Thought to Be

They always thought that I was this Negro. How insulting? What an insult! However, they came to realize that I am the Negus after their spirits ceased to be damned and came down on earth. How ironic? Will they come to the realization one day that I am God? Time will tell. Only time will tell.

The Core Tenets Shall Not Be Transgressed

The natural law.

Knowledge.

Self-respect.

Identity.

Respect for our forebears.

It Never Ends

It never ends, human beings killing each other like wild and angry beasts. Are we doomed by nature and destiny despite some great accomplishments? Insanity at its very best, sad to confess and see.

Still Spinning in Dizziness

Both of their minds, his and hers, are still spinning in dizziness and confusion by considering me to be someone I am not, a Negro. I am the Negus, and not just any Negus, a renegade one. Never dare to put your dirty hands or handcuffs on me. I am not one of your many stolen properties and lands. I am the Renegade Negus by destiny and birth literary.

They Can Refuse to Think

They can gladly refuse to think that is their problem, and we will not think for them. We will only think how best to destroy them.

As I Walk in This Universe

As I walk in this universe, I find my role to be extremely delicate, very meaningful, and profound. I reflect on every day.

Deep Down

Deep down, I don't fret too much because I know and can feel that destiny is always in the process of taking its course. I know this by experience.

I Have Wishes

I have wishes and God has a plan. Whatever the plan is, says the religious man, I will accept and submit unfaithfully.

Transgressed

He has transgressed not some rather all the principles of reasonability countless times. Therefore, his demise ought to be implemented by guillotine only.

Empty Speeches

Empty speeches and the show continues. What else is there to say or argue about?

Why Don't You Believe?

In it simplest form, the question is, why don't you believe?

I did until I found out everything was and is a forgery, a farce. Do you want me to betray the truth by validating lies and insanity? Don't they have too many clients already?

In Death

While breathing, I am not. They do not consider me to be. However, in death, I will become the Mystic. I was and I am always the Mystic. Nothing has ever changed, but they have changed our to view me and appreciate the value of the legacy.

Happiness

I find immense pleasure in small things of great value and meaning. Surprisingly, they find theirs in criminality. Should I try criminality then? I ponder.

They Are Applauding

They are applauding foolishness with great excitement to my surprise, and this is not even theater and cinema. Am I dreaming? Are they forced to applaud? Or are they free men and women? Fascinating indeed!

I Can Move in Mediocrity

I can move in mediocrity; rather I choose not to. Thus, I move in excellence and extraordinary states of mind.

What Happened?

What happened? You used to be a man of character and conviction.

Well, the full story is extremely difficult to explain; just know that I woke up in hell in front of the devil. Furthermore, he lectured me to some degree about power and darkness. That is all there is to know.

Is this the reason you are drowning in darkness and sins? Could you still be saved? My questions were met with a dark silence. I needed to figure out things of divine, celestial, and holy nature rapidly to at least save his soul if the possibility remains.

The Truest Warriors

The truest warriors always have loyalty no matter what and always depart this earth as loyalists whether the cause is righteous or not.

What Do You See?

Whenever you look at me, what do you see?
Whenever you look at me, what do you feel?

Whenever you look at me, what do you question? What don't you question?

Are you trustworthy beyond the point of ordinary loyalty?

I beg to know.

I Find Life

I find life to be meaningful and absurd simultaneously. That is the recipe for greatness and disaster. This dichotomy is known to be true. Can the idea of perfection be considered absurd at the origin and throughout?

I Command!

I command! Let her ride her luck for the time being so we can all see where it ends if it does.

I Am Entering the Space

Mentally and spiritually, I am entering the space of the deity; henceforth, all things and living matters shall wait.

I Am Not Here...

I am not here to heal rather to teach and heal the psyche of mankind if need be. Only if need be and I insist.

I Think

I think your mind will appreciate a little bit of silliness and stupidity in order to release the tension. Please relax and appreciate the comedy.

Impenetrable

Impenetrable, so do not dare to try your luck because you will be defeated and may face death on your journey of stubbornness and defiance. Only imbeciles refuse to learn when necessary.

Wherever Darkness Is...

Wherever darkness is, light and enlightenment shall shine with full power and force.

Please Send the Mystic Signal

Please send the mystic signal.

Well, not yet. The African gods, the African ancestors, and the African counsels all have not spoken yet nor debated these matters. Only them do the authority rests upon, and they will when they deem the time is mostly appropriate. Don't fret! There is no need to.

I Beg You to Listen

I beg you to listen silently and attentively to your friends and enemies. They are going to teach you valuable lessons about betrayal and loyalty. If you live in heaven, you don't have to, but if the earth is your home, you must.

Extremism

The seeds of extremism are being planted in full light, and no one gives a damn. The logic dictates that death must follow and they will act surprise, clueless, with extraordinary ignorance. Who damned these sinners? Is God or the force of darkness the author? Don't they walk around with fundamental erroneous religious beliefs? To be a human is highly a fascinating experience in every level of reasonability.

Fascinated with Darkness

They are always fascinated with darkness.

Can't they be fascinated by light and enlightenment?

Can't they be fascinated with both light and darkness?

Why darkness only?

I guess they will never see light and enlightenment maybe in death.

Who knows?

These Rights

Are these rights embedded in nature for all or just the few?

Do these principles apply to all or just the very few?

Since these answers are obvious, I resist to answer.

Inside the Mind of a Genius

Inside the mind of a genius, only God can see and predict maybe evil as well if permitted.

Misjudgment

Their success is being attributed to their extraordinary skills, but they possess none. I attribute this to the circumstance of their birth, the weight of history, their many privileges including their ability to deceive and steal. Thus, misjudgment is everywhere you look if you dare to because with all this good fortune and wealth, they are still crooks. In all logic, can their conscience rest at night? May God save their soul, I pray.

Mesmerizing

The contractions are mesmerizing to the brink of insanity.

Points of View

Those points of view may well be stupid as hell or smart as heaven; still the author has a natural right to them. Be the judge if so deemed. I won't.

How Do You See the Universe?

How do you see the universe?
   I see it in God's eyes.
   How do you see the universe?
   Well, I see it in the devil's eyes.
   Well, no wonder we are in trouble. Is this the balance we
never sought?
   Dramatic indeed!

In Darkness

In darkness, they soar; and in light, they shrink.
   What is wrong?
   What am I missing?
   What is their problem?
   I don't have answers to these questions.
   Do you, God?
   Can you explain?

I Am a Stranger

With certainty, I am just a stranger in this strange place. Furthermore, I am trying extremely hard to understand this strange place marked only by darkness and miseries while keeping an open mind. My mind and heart are filled with sadness, pity, and incomprehension. I wish I had a solution to eradicate all this.

Raped Mind

They raped my mind of all its valuable history, then filled it with bullshit, treachery, and falsehood, and I learned this inside and outside of the education system. No kidding! Contrary to many facts, they have the audacity to deny everything and rewrite history. Now, I am trying my very best to recover whatever I can. No wonder I am lost in darkness. With all their audacity intact, they claim all our greatness with a straight face. Dear God, can you see our tears turned to anger?

Hell, can you liberate their souls or should I ask God instead?

They Turn Their Backs on God

They say that they are extremely exhausted for praying to God without tangible results. Therefore, they decided to turn their backs on God. Will God punish them with fury or forgive them with kindness? Who knows? I dare not to interpret God's will, answer, kindness, or fury, others may.

They Are the Makers

They are the sole makers of their mental incompetence, misfortune, and corruption due to their lack of courage to stand up for what is righteous, and they dare to complain about everything. Not amused by the theater.

Democracy

Despite the fact that this is a democracy, if we cannot convince them by logic and reason, then democracy must cease its existence temporary or permanently so they can be condemned without the rule of law. Or secession ought to be declared; therefore, guns shall speak the language of death once for all to settle these profound differences.

I Am Not Good

I am not good at things of foreign and strange nature by nature. Therefore, don't dare to nurture me. Call me close-minded if so wished, and I accept.

I Am Expressing the Very Best of Mankind

I am expressing the very best of mankind, and I accept the worst without expressing it ever.

I am Not on a Mission

I am not a man on a mission, rather just a gentleman travelling on the pace of destiny to fulfill its meaning.

Nothing Is an Accident

Nothing is an accident. Everything you pass through or everything that passes you by has a purpose. You may certainly not understand this at the present, but later in your journey before death, you will. Please try your very best to be a good citizen of the universe despite the challenges.

The Art of Creativity

Look at everything, consider all possibilities, and finally, disqualify those who are worthless. That is the art of creativity at its core with the ability of retaining only the extraordinary. Needless to say, this process is challenging.

It Was Meant in Poor Taste

It was meant in poor taste, but since he bears the mark of imbecility, unsurprisingly, he cannot just get it. The lesson is do not condemn your mind to ignorance.

Incredulity at Its Peak

Her stubbornness has reached the point of incredulity and insanity because others believe; instead, I showed her God standing next to her. Not only she did not believe but she had the audacity to question me and God. Her questioning was met with silence. Then, we simply vanished as a smoke in the air.

They Can Choose

They certainly can choose even have a right to play in the mud. I choose to stay clean, reach, and converse with things and living matters of celestial and holy nature.

There Is No Hate in My Heart

The force of darkness is asking me to burn them with hate for their committed crimes and lies. My response, there is no hate in my heart.

Trapped in Hell

They are trying to trap me in hell, ignoring that the spirit of my ancestors and the spirit of God travel within like oxygen in my veins.

Dare to Tell You

They will dare to tell you all the things you cannot do without telling you what you can. If creativity comes to you naturally, then ignore that advice for whatever it is worth.

I Beg Not to Be Disturbed

I beg not to be disturbed due to the fact that I am watching the greatest political show on the brink of insanity. This is the greatest theater of all but of bad taste in the echelon of absurdity and grandeur. Others seem to enjoy this theater, and that is not absurd at all until unfunny decisions are taken to precisely affect their lives. Are you sure that democracy is still worth the pain of insanity? Until mankind's mind is perfected, the answer is affirmative. Furthermore, this burden of perfection and other demands can be left at the doorstep of heaven and hell, so both masters cannot claim ignorance. Objectively, we cannot escape but ponder. What and who did enable us to reach this point of calamity? If and only if the answer is truthful maybe, just maybe we will be able to objectively remedy the situation or this mess.

Timing

Destiny is a matter of timing conceived in a world of blindness until we walk the path.

Just a Difference of Opinion

This is just a difference of opinion supported by the basic law of nature. Therefore, war is needless.

I Have a Free Soul

I have a free soul. Simply meaning neither God nor the spirit of obscurantism can buy it, too valuable and priceless to sell. You have to have a free soul to navigate these matters of darkness and enlightenment. Don't you agree? Does it matter?

I Claim

I claim ignorance in all things presented to me; therefore, pardon my ignorance with kindness and compassion.

It Only Takes a Revolutionary Mind

In all honesty, we can never look at this insanity and be at ease in our minds and souls. It only takes a revolutionary mind to understand my concerns to its deepest core. It is written somewhere in heaven and hell that those who must die shall. However, the revolution must happen once for all. My hope is to address all these grievances so we don't have to revisit them and revisit death in the same manner.

This Universe

This universe has given me so much joy and pain simultaneously that I am at a lost to characterize all this by reason. Thus, I dare not to. I only wait for my demise in a golden silence and observation while travelling in the galaxy.

I Beg Ignorance

Please don't condemn me I beg ignorance of the law and don't plead guilty. Isn't this reasonable enough for the court by reason of ignorance? If this is unsatisfactory, thus, I claim insanity for my defense. If this is still unsatisfactory, there must be a trick in the law because there always is. I know this by observation only. A crooked lawyer must have written that law anyway. Can't you tell with certainty? Therefore, where is the trick?

Trying to Understand Life

In trying to understand death, I am trying to comprehend the meaning of life not define it.

Turmoil and Wars

I live in a universe of turmoil, chaos, death, and wars, many distances away from paradise. Thus, my present to this universe is *The Birth of Fine Art*.

Follow Your Own Path

Please follow your own path to heaven, and I will follow mine to hell, vice versa. Don't you know the meaning of liberty? If God created mankind with a free will, the fundamental question rests upon humanity to ask. Who are you to deny others liberty, the spirit of darkness, a crook, or a government? Don't dare to preach to me! Save your own soul; mine is safe like an unreachable and unseen bunker. God knows including the spirit of darkness. My soul is surrounded by righteousness and enlightenment. From time to time, the spirit of darkness knocks and is sent back to hell countless times where it belongs. Savor the fire!

How Come...

How come you cannot find your way to heaven while I find mine to hell so easily? Maybe heaven does not exist; only hell does, so come join us in hell.

Do you really have a choice? Isn't this the only option left? Unfathomable indeed!

Let us stay curious. Our hope is that our curiosity will eventually lead us to heaven; if not we will have to imagine it.

My Lineage

My lineage has always been marked by defiance, righteousness, and critical and radical thinking; therefore, the only remaining reasonable option is to carry the torch with full conviction. Damn Black fists in the air, Negus!

Natural Power

"As you probably know by now, I have given you extraordinary natural power, and don't abuse it in any circumstance," says God. "I am God, and I will take care of your enemies. Whether you feel me spiritually or not, whether you see me or not, whether you believe or not, whether you ponder or not, whether you seek forgiveness or not, whether you question me or not, whether you seek enlightenment or not, my status is I am and never cease to be despite all else. Not all things are meant to be understood for your own sake. Ignorance is the best medicine in some cases, not all."

The Dead

The misery of humanity is blatantly untenable even the dead are crying. Can you see their tears?

The misery of humanity is blatantly untenable even the dead are speaking even thought dead. Can you hear them?

Listen attentively and see for yourself because nobody will translate for those alive.

Death Will Come

It is written somewhere in destiny with certainty that death will come peacefully or violently whether we wish it or not. Furthermore, if ever death has a wish, we can conclude with certainty that death's wish is always granted no matter what.

They Don't Want Us to Speak Out

They don't want us to speak out and if we cannot speak now,
    when can we?
    When are we allowed to?
    Do we really need their permission?
    Even God knows we have been granted free will.
    How dare they, is the question?
    They cannot even acknowledge their own ills, so let us
remind them their insanity.
    They have a tendency of forgetting who we truly are,
but we don't.

Nothing to Sell

I have nothing to sell, but the force of darkness wants my
soul. Go to hell and savor your own fire! My soul cannot
be found nor bought because it moves in infinity, celestial,
and holy nature.

I Have No Intent

I have no intent to tell the absolute truth just lies. Come
to your own conclusion if so deemed. This is not a big deal

because life will not come to a stop. It keeps rolling both ways in hell and heaven. What is the fuss? There shall be none, but there is. I ponder why.

I Don't Plan to Die in Silence

I don't plan to die in silence; even God will say that I have betrayed one of the most fundamental principles of knowledge, decency, and courage while facing insanity.

Why should I die in silence?

Even God will be surprised.

Is there nothing to critique? I am not in the aphasia state. Therefore, hell must tremble at its core and shock waves must be sent. I have been granted the mission by destiny. This goes back before birth, during birth, and after birth, I carry that mystical torch no matter how heavy or light.

I Will Behave

I will behave if they do. If they fire, I will fire back as I must, and the volcano must rise literary and mystically.

Defined by Color Only Not So Fast!

I am falsely defined and accused by color only inside and outside the court, inside and outside of several malls, inside and outside of logic, inside and outside of the crooked judiciary madness by the racists. The racists always define me by color only. What a surprise! How do I explain and convince them that I am the origin. I am the birth of humanity. My mind, spirit, and soul decide against any reasonable explanation because there is no inch of light inside those darkish minds. At their very best, they are savages, crooks, impostors, murderers, prophets of hell, and exploiters who want to teach morality. Disturbing indeed! These are not just meaningless words put together for the sake of fiction because facts are lying in and outside of your conscience if you still have any left. Does the truth hurt? Our mutual rendezvous is in hell. Wish it doesn't exist; then, I will depart for heaven afterward.

Can you confirm your mandatory attendance?

Will your absence be charged and reprimanded with contempt of the divine court?

Can you see and comprehend at some point, the brilliance of the original man?

Can you pay your dues without doing everything in your irrational power to implement our demise? In your many own writings and falsehood, you repeatedly say that you cannot hear nor find our voices of resistance during slavery;

meanwhile we were delighted to sell, even negotiate the price. You cannot understand our feelings because those feelings and voices are unknown or muted to this present day. I think you still possess your hearing sense. You can hear me now, can't you? Or should I scream? Record this one in your book of truths. It seems to me that you have another for lies, and the book of truths is always burned afterward. Meanwhile, the one for lies is always kept and offered for study. Can we conclude that your book of lies is taught as a cult of superiority for all to see and revere? Don't forget the rendezvous! Sadly, you have multiple tendencies to forget that the damn Black fists of Negus have never been down even against nature since the commencement of all things or challenges.

Is this mental state aphasia?

How do you call it or explain this in your own words?

Not so fast! I am not a Negro. I am a renegade. I am the Negus straight from heaven and the land of the birth of humanity.

Do you want specific reference? Somewhere in the Kongo Kingdom you will find my history, the history of my ancestry written without any fear. Sit back and watch me soar in divinity. Here we are! Here we stand! With the power of a great volcano ready to unleash the lava, here we stand as defiant as ever. Never forget in peace or war our Black fists never rest. Our spirit always travels continuously to unlock the mystic.

They Are Demanding the Truth

They are demanding the truth and justice inside the wrong places. I reminded them that this is theater inside a theater, and I was disturbed.

Did they stop to object and interject?

Of course not, they were kicked out to the amusement of the theater.

Expose Me

Expose me objectively to all things of rational and irrational nature so I will do my very best to understand and consider their meaning. If I can't, I can't. If I can, I will show my deepest appreciation.

I Never Meant

My apologies, I never meant to imply the truth because I don't know what the truth is. I meant to imply the contrary. Don't you agree? If not, can you read my mind?

The Spirit of Darkness

Silence please! The spirit of darkness is travelling at the highest speed in my mind as we speak, and I need to capture it, her, or him. I don't know how best to characterize this. Where's God? Help please!

The Angels

The angels are descending on earth to study. and I never meant to rob them, but I did just to give them a taste of the earth. Of course, they were appalled and surprised; some of them came against their wish and will.

You see! Even in heaven there is no such thing as democracy. Thus, how could this place called heaven be perfect?

Aim

Aim not to offend rather please, my dear.

Not to Offend

Aim not to offend, my dear, the future is too demanding, as a result, I can't accommodate your many caprices. Still offended?

They Will Ask

They will ask, and I will only answer after my demise.

Dismiss Me

Dismiss me in case you don't like me, but I caution against dismissing my ideas because they are worthy of consideration. Since you are blinded by irrationality, I highly doubt if you do, still I offer my advice even if unwelcome.

Got to Make It Right

Got to make it right by all means of reason and rationality.
    If we can't, we plead for God's assistance.
    If there is no God, are we doomed with certainty?

Are We Claiming Anything?

To my knowledge, we don't claim to be the very best, but statistics are.

Are we claiming anything?

Of course not. We don't need to if interested go speak with statistics.

Insurmountable Oddness

How come are we the only race on earth to face double hell, on earth and hell? What is happening, God? Do you want the list of crimes and injustices committed against us? Did you lose control of your creation? Do you even exist as I deeply ponder? Insurmountable oddness, but we beat them, not always. Can you assist?

A World of Imagination

They are trying and succeeding in building a world that resembles their doomed imagination. A world constructed on lies and chaos. The uncharacteristic case, philosophy, dogma, or whatever is built on reason of insanity and dominance by all irrational means necessary. Unfathomable! Pity! Doomed! Our discontent shall be unmistaken, written in black and white for all to see. If not yet, well! They will be tortured mentally because they have human blood in their conscience and hands.

Who Is Counting?

Who is counting their deaths? Who should? Their deaths are meaningless; meanwhile, they are counting the deaths of animals. Implying that the deaths of animals are worthy of careful attention and consideration. Doomed and damned with certainty they shall be!

School Us with Lies

School us with lies, and we will school you with a golden silence. Hope you can understand it.

Not Bearing the Oath

Not bearing the oath of the past. Don't need to, don't have to; I am creating something unique for the future.

Our Slogan

Our slogan is not change; rather, rethink the future for the sake of country. Otherwise stated, for the sake of country rethink the future.

Where Did They Cook Those Great Lies?

Where did they cook those great lies? People are devouring them with great appetite.

I honestly don't know. I am not one of them.

Where did you cook these great lies?

We cooked them in hell. Where else could we have cooked them? Are you satisfied?

The question is met with great silence only.

Can't You Be Kind?

Can't you be kind with your words?

Kind? Nope! I cannot be. Have you seen their crimes? I speak, but I don't kill. They kill with or without secrecy, then have the audacity to brandish any law that favors and justifies their insanity, their folly. If they don't have it on their books, they simply say, "Fuck it!" My place is to critique only; theirs is to critique and kill as illustrated factually. Check for yourself and be amused, be amazed with the possibility to be damned and doomed. Why not?

Aren't You Surprised?

Aren't you surprised?
Of course not! I am dealing with humanity, am I not?
Don't imply anything else!
Isn't this a true statement, is it?
I will elaborate further if and only if deemed necessary.

They Fought

They fought and died fearlessly for irrationality and insane principles. How come?

I don't know. I am too far away removed from their reality, therefore unable to comprehend the driving force behind their motives.

There Is No Need

There is no need to fret. I was born to navigate these incertitudes in full confidence.

The Observer

The observer never speaks; his only duty is to observe rationality, irrationality, morality, immorality, vice, greatness, the mystic, the absurdities of existence while we exist. This point must be emphasized; no matter what he never speaks on anything just absorbs all things and living matters. As a result, humanity finds him to be strange and fascinating simultaneously; in return, he never reveals his thoughts on humanity or anything else for that matter. Multiple theories and conclusions are assessed by humanity; none is revealed by the observer. We cannot escape but ask. Who is he?

Don't You…?

Don't you want to hear the truth?

Doesn't your mind want to be free?

Of course not! The truth is not pretty.

How are you going to build the future?

The future will be built on lies. I know it sounds absurd to ask, but this conversation is absurd to me.

Are you satisfied?

You don't get it, do you?

I meant to say, "Get the fuck out here!" Leave me at peace the moralizer. Who convinced you that I need to be moralized? God? Evil? Both? I simply enjoy the absurdities of existence while I exist. I am not the first one nor will I be the last. Keep screaming moralization of the universe! Moralization of the earth!

Do you need a microphone? I have a damaged one. Oh! The megaphone is damaged too. You can have both.

Do you want to moralize hell as well?

What about baptizing the head of hell with the water of darkness? Fuck out here! Don't you have anything better to do? Huh? Huh!

Nothing else needs to be said or argued; only silence should summarize all things, all mystics.

I Want Power

I want power to do evil, not good, power that comes straight from hell.

Gracefully I Decline

Gracefully I decline to serve, serve humanity in any capacity. I think they are capable of serving themselves in all capacities. May the spirit of our ancestors and may the spirit of God always shine on all of them with great care, grace, and inspiration for the virtue and greatness of humanity.

By the Grace of God

By the grace of God, I can't be you only advice, can't walk in your shoes. Please be well and consider my advice with care and respect. I wish you the best regardless.

You Have a Very Bad Tendency

You have a very bad tendency of forgetting who I was, using the past tense as if I cease to exist. Is a reintroduction necessary? I don't think so. Should I restate my name to refresh your memory? Nope! No need to. I never was even in my demise. I never cease to exist spiritually. How many times do you want me to reintroduce myself to you? Listen to nature! Listen to the wind. Listen to the sea. Observe the stars. Look inside the universe. I float in infinity. Do you know that I navigate the universe differently, be it physically or spiritually? Does the mystical universe exist to you? Whether or not, I never cease to be like an invisible shadow of righteousness, and I am always floating in infinity. Henceforth, I never cease to be.

You Are Seeking Respect

You are seeking respect where respect is not due. You have the audacity to stand in front of me with a defiant look and attitude as if you are some kind of queen. However, the reality of the situation begs mercy and forgiveness due to the fact that you are just a simple bitch with arrogance facing an arrogant and proud man. Can you read me? Do you really know me? Do you really know where my spirit rests? Pity! Absurdities of existence while I exist! If you only knew, but you will never know nor comprehend my destiny. Why I was given birth? Let the case rests without further elaboration.

Those Self-Declared Enemies

Those self-declared enemies, I possess the ultimate power to destroy them, but I won't. They should thank my dear parents for raising me differently. I will even send flowers to their coffins with a real deep sorrow of humility and regret expressed truthfully.

I Will Pray

Truthfully, I will pray for heaven to open its doors wide open for them, despite their criminality and multiple sins. However, only God shall be able to forgive them and no expectation must be raised.

Admiration for Mankind

The master of hell claims admiration for mankind, and he wants as many people to visit hell as possible. When did hell become a tourist destination? When did hell become a destination of enjoyment and relaxation? Thus, he is claiming that mankind is being tricked by his own imagination and God, that hell is not as worst as portrayed by both mankind's and God's imaginations.

Highly intriguing indeed!

What a surprise!

If hell is not as bad as portrayed by our imagination, thus, why don't you enjoy hell by yourself, master of hell?

We will greatly be appreciative of this possibility. We will appreciate the peace of mind specially, after our demise.

Are You Sure?

Please don't cry or worry about me. I am safe in hell.

Are you sure of your location? It sounds like paradise.

Are you being held for ransom in hell? This is something never heard of.

The communication has been disconnected.

I Am Tempted

I am tempted to believe to a power greater than me.

What about yourself?

Well, I am tempted to disagree respectfully. And let's not bring this uncomfortable conversation further for the sake of our friendship.

Agreed!

You Are in Safe Arms

You are in safe arms. Therefore, you need to trust me because I will protect you to death if need be. No need to doubt my truest intentions.

How Would You Like to Die?

The question is put in its simplest form.

How would you like to die, in bravery or cowardliness?

I don't know. You tell me, master of hell!

No Need to Fret

Not need to fret; you are travelling with God even though you cannot see him. You are invisible to the head of hell. Your destiny is too meaningful and extremely valuable. It goes without saying that I indeed trust God by faith with my being both spiritual and physical.

In All Honesty

In all honesty, I like the seriousness of the matter because it brings the very best out of me in another state of mind.

This Madness

This madness is personal to me and let me handle this. I will turn hell upside down if need be. Volcanoes must rise if necessary. Only silence is required, and let the transition and transformation to another state of mind and spirit begin. Nothing else shall be revealed.

Things of Another Nature

Things of another nature are created in absolute silence, which will make hell tremble. The process cannot be revealed for the sake of mystery.

Trustworthy or Not

Trustworthy or not, events will only reveal your truest character. You are not shielded as you may think you are. The mask will eventually come down or not.

The Knowledge I Carry

The knowledge I carry is of celestial and holy nature. Can you be trusted with it? Are you certain that you are not going to betray God, the gods? Needless to say, the final outcome is known but not revealed until it happens.

Please Exercise Caution

Please exercise extreme caution and sound judgment with the given power. Do not disappoint and justify excuses in any circumstance. Your own soul shall be the last entity to judge the seriousness of the situation before any action is taken.

The Logic

The logic is extremely simple and basic.
No faith, no present.
No faith, no marriage.
No faith, no trust.
No faith, no basic understanding.
No faith no existence.
At the end, no faith, no God.
You have everything you need. Even though you are unable to see it for the time being. Thus, please use your faith. If you cannot, the question is, do you carry a dead soul within? When in doubt, your faith shall carry you through only if you believe.

Pained

Pained by the mistrust and relieved of the duty of honesty.

Virtue

Pained by mistrust but not relieved of the duty of virtue or honesty.

Quite Uncharacteristic

Quite uncharacteristic to be amused and moved by virtue. Not amused at all! Considering a civilized world. To the contrary, I will be.

In an Uncivilized Universe

In an uncivilized universe, nothing must come as a surprise. All must be expected without a shock of morality.

Can't You Tell?

Did they buy his conscience and soul or what?

Can't you tell? Aren't you smart enough to tell? If not, ask for advice and guidance.

The Possibilities Are

The possibilities are our path may diverge and never converge again, diverge and converge again. Whatever the outcome, destiny will tell. At peace, I am.

The Snake

The snake tried to lure me into wrong, but its head was cut off before any attempt. Seen that coming from miles away.

The Don

For some reasons unknown to me but known to them, they are trying to confuse me with the original gangster (OG). However, I am not, simply too brilliant to be. I am the Don. Consider this literally or figuratively, whichever is your preference. Undercover I stay.

The Score

The score must be settled right here, right now, to this present day. No further consideration is allowed. My patience has run its course. We must settle the score in our own terms, only our own terms, and they can go to hell and rejoice.

My Apologies

My deepest apologies are expressed because I cannot claim things that don't belong to me. I am not from Europe. Don't they claim the universe, heaven, even hell for themselves, only themselves? Don't believe me; just look at the facts, even their own facts and actions. These will tell you everything you need to know including all you can never grasp. Don't believe me; just look at best or with fury how they loot the universe, heaven, hell, what else I know, and what else I don't know. What about those damned Arabs? Are you forgetting them? Of course not, they are in the same boat just wearing different garments and religion for differentiation purpose only with the same goal of hegemony. How can I forget about them? Yeah! Those damn Arabs! Didn't they sell us in Zanzibar and many other places, then have the audacity to murder us and steal our land? Did I claim aphasia? How can I convert to their religion and stay in this madness while being the Negus that I am? Impossible!

Who has ever walked or set feet in this universe first?

I am too ignorant to know the response to such a complex question, so I am still pondering.

How come they claim superiority and divinity on all things seen and unseen?

Why don't you ask them?

Do you need to locate them by region, religion?

Do you need their geographical coordinates?

Don't you have a global positioning system at hand and ready to go?

At this point, the point is well driven and addressed. No need to elaborate further. Intriguing indeed for the looters! Not so intriguing indeed for the victims!

Silence from heaven and hell!

Nobody will be happy, and nobody is anyway. The only question is, Where are they going to crucify me? Will it be at a different place than Lumumba?

Dare to touch me, and you will see the ghost and die in misery. No need to fret, and allow me to float in infinity. I always do without permission of heaven including hell. I always float in infinity.

We Don't See Eye to Eye

We don't see eye to eye nor believe in peace. Nonetheless, we see eye to eye in war and the need to massacre each other; I mean the destruction of humanity. And we are too far away to be qualified as savages, murderers. Of course, we are not. We don't need civility, and don't dare to remind us.

Even heaven and hell don't see eye to eye for how long? Do you know with certainty?

To say the least, we are just humans. Cut us some slack. Would you? Why wouldn't you?

Problems

Problems are everywhere and no solution is to be found anywhere, just opinions, many opinions without a result. What is the rationale, if I may ask politely?

Just to Be

What is the coolest thing to be?

None! Just to be.

As the great William Shakespeare says, "To be or not to be."

Extremely Urgent

Please, this matter is extremely urgent, and I cannot stress the urgency of the matter enough. Please call God and the master of hell together. I need to speak in their presence. In case they are sleeping, they shall be awaken immediately. I hope not due to the fact that my desire is not to put any kind of discomfort to their respective pain of sleep if they haven't any already. No message is to be left. I need to speak to them directly, says the unknown and unidentified spirit. The highest confidentiality is required.

Died in Disgrace Buried in Honor

Died in disgrace buried in honor, he was a crooked politician. Nothing invented, just an observation. With this honor, my mind cannot escape but ask. Was he honored in heaven or hell or both simultaneously as well? I guess we will never know.

Not Only Do They Wish

Not only do they wish but as well as implement miseries in my life. I don't know who told them that I am happy.

Probably my many miseries still make them unhappy; thus, they need more and more implemented. From what kind of hell did they originate? Is it the same one all of us reference? Strange indeed! How can I trick them?

She Cannot Be Faulted

She cannot be faulted because this kind of outcome is written somewhere in destiny, heaven, and hell.

She Thought She Could

She thought she could trick my mind, and I knew that she could not. Therefore, I let the narrative develop so we all can see the outcome. Here she was, trapped in hell and lies. How sad! Well, Just another soul trapped in hell to make the hell master content.

If and Only If...

If and only if people's intentions come from hell and heaven, assuming this logic to be true, the simple question is, why shouldn't I assume the very best and the worst in humanity? Isn't this logical and reasonable? It is true that from time to time I will be wrong.

Your Imagination

Your imagination is only limited by your ability to think outside of the many barriers set by society. Your imagination can break them or stay inside. The decision is yours to figure out.

This Needs to Be Asked

Are you okay?

Never been better! Fine like the Negus! Fine like the maestro of maestri.

Sir! Have we seen all things from you?

Not yet, sir! Just not yet! The end of the final chapter may never be written.

I Would Like…

I would like to see your stunning beauty every time I wake up. I need your kindness to keep my heart warm and your simple gestures of grace, care, and humility as a reminder of goodness in mankind despite all else. Goddess you are.

Heroism

Heroism is never meant for me, nor do I seek it. That explains the reason I move in silence and under the radar. The fact of the matter is I was born to fulfill a specific destiny, a destiny of righteousness.

Consideration

Greatness is not the only noun taken into consideration. Mediocrity is considered as well in forging my path into the status of greatness. Is the voyage enjoyable?

All the Rights

How come the government has all the rights to commit murder of foreigners including of its own citizens and I have none? I mean none literally, not even for self-defense against the government. Every single time the government knocks at my door, the memories of my demise are refreshed. I am a tortured man.

Elected

I was elected in a democracy, not dictatorship. However, expect dictatorship. Correct! You heard this correctly, and your mind did not trick you. Am I the first elected official to contradict himself, to change the course of politicking or history? If interested in honesty, I think you can answer this question with ease.

Aren't you interested in honesty?

How and why should we expect dictatorship instead of democracy, sir?

The fact of the matter is democracy does not make sense as we speak; just listen to the noise and complaints. Thus, I will implement dictatorship, and by the time I leave, I will leave you with a great legacy. If and only if dictatorship is unsatisfactory to great lengths then, I will return the country to a democratic system. Isn't this rationale?

Just Found Out

Surprisingly, they just found out that he is not clever as he pretended, to their discontent. I knew this along the way in silence.

Give Me Death

Give me death for my convictions, my discontent for crimes, and injustices committed against us, and I will be content, content to fulfill destiny.

Contract

I was sent and given the power to negotiate the following contract by God, not to change anything else, and I do intend to follow the specific instructions given to me by God. Please do not be deviant from these commands unless you want to invite enormous trouble and catastrophes to your doors.

Healthy Noise

We need a healthy noise in a democracy; if the noise ceases, you ought to worry and rise before you wake up in a kingdom, a forgery by birthright introduced, imposed by bloodshed and falsehood.

The Ocean, the Sea

The ocean, the sea, since I cannot trust mankind to tell me about the history of slavery, I want to learn it from you, from your tears, from the Black blood mixed with your waters, from your collections of the truth buried at the bottom of your waters, from your collections of the dead, not from those who have committed the most horrifying crimes in the history of mankind unmatched in savageness and evil. I am listening attentively and weeping for all the dead, all of them without fault, condemnation, nor blame as far as they are concerned.

If I Could…

If I could command, I will. If I could dictate, I will. Underestimate me at your own peril.

They Don't Revere Weakness

They don't revere weakness, just power, and they will be surprised to learn what they cannot see nor understand.

A Mind of a Certain Caliber

I need a mind of a certain caliber.

What for?

This cannot be explained nor discussed and it ought to remain a myth.

The Business of the State

The business of the state must go on despite all else, despite the assassinations, the dead, the sellouts, and the war against us. Let the brave men, women, and children of this dear country stand up in resistance against evil. The message is simple; we don't retreat, and we will fight them to the doorstep of hell and inside. They are going to face nothing else except death. Write this in capital letters in heaven and hell if so wished.

The Intent

The intent was never to tell the truth but to deceive, so if this is not satisfactory to you as I can assume it is to me, get over it! I do intend to address you an apology in the near future, and time will heal your dissatisfaction. Trust me, it always does. Do you want flowers as well? Do you want to die a bitter man? Don't you want to forgive people who have done you wrong before death and ask for your own forgiveness? I know you will. Life is a routine of sins and righteousness, sins against righteousness.

Earned

Earned by sweat, tears, blood, courage, discipline, hard work, not given.

Given

Given, not earned. Go figure the rest!

They Won't Understand

They won't understand. As a result, why pain myself to death to explain?

Courage of Opinions

I have the courage of my opinions. Do you?

May God Send Death

If I am unable to think critically, may God send death.

Trajectory

In my trajectory, I met with evil. He/she tried to destroy me to no avail. Prepared I was, blessed I am, I always travel with the gods and God. This is a matter of destiny. Never dare to try me once more! This is the only warning available.

Failure

Never be afraid to fail. Have the courage to fail because only failure can lead you to greatness and great creativity.

Dare to trust your own instincts.

Dare to take your imagination to uncommon places, places unknown to any other mankind, appreciate and value the unique gift, the gift of reason, the gift to reason, the gift of enlightenment.

You Can Never Understand

You can never understand my anger until you walk in my emotions, until you see what I have seen, until you understand the lies, forgeries, murders, atrocities, injustices committed against us. So abstain of any judgment. Whether they wear black or white skin, whether they wear black and white faces alternatively, our enemies must fall, must fall by their own sins, must fall by their own sword.

Superior

Is there anything else, any other kind superior to Black or Negus?

Nope! There is none or any other kind, nor do I suggest the contrary. Please refer to science if in doubt of any kind.

I Am Listening

I am listening to the great Ludwig Van Beethoven's fifth symphony for the curiosity of creativity, for the curiosity of the mind including the deepest appreciation of the genius composition. The demand of my mind ought to be satisfied in noncomplex mathematical equations.

Can We Trust Them?

Can we trust them with the simple truth?

Of course not! Haven't you learned anything else worth questioning from them?

I Don't Mean

I don't mean to challenge human logic, but I am going to because I operate on another spiritual level. Just watch me be bold as ever.

Give Me That Power

Give me that power, and I will abuse it. Why not? Look around you. What do you see?

Hero revered, hero betrayed.

Hero by forgery, hero revered.

Hero today, villain tomorrow, I am.

Not My Aim

Failure is not my aim; only success is. Fret if so desired. I don't need to.

Weak Minds

Many weak minds are going to fall for those lies, then justify them. Meanwhile the enlightened are going to resist those lies by speaking the truth with courage at all cost.

Not My Concern

Average is not my concern. Greatness at a unique dimension is.

Why?

Why don't you trust this bitch but trust this well-mannered lady?

The answer should be apparent even to the blind and deaf. If not, please use all your senses. One is unworthy of such honor and privilege, and the other is.

The General

I am the distinguished general. I always lead and command my troops with poise in the battlefield while battling death and uncertainties. All is written in hell and heaven, and all we do is to fulfill destiny as humans. Dead they must be.

Please Travel with Me

Please travel with me, not physically, rather spiritually, and I will show you the full power and strength of a Negus.

Here We Meet Again

Here we meet again, this time in hell. Are you going to have the audacity to lie to me again? Do you care about your fate even in hell or all is lost?

Should I Free You?

Should I free you from your own lies?
    Or will you be able to free yourself?

Distracted

Heaven is being distracted by hell.
Should we worry?
Should the earth worry?

Orders

Orders from heaven, sir. Here they are.
Please send them back.
Yes, sir!
Here they are, orders from hell.
Please send them back. Tell heaven and hell that I have questions concerning the imperfection of the universe, and these questions are not being answered in a satisfactory manner. Until then, I don't take orders.

The Earth

The world is a troubled place.
Where do you find the strength to navigate these trouble waters?
I find the strength in the spiritual aspect of life like many others.

This Must Be Understood

This must be understood. I don't stand up against evil, not just like any man. I stand up against evil as a Black man, as a renegade Negus. Never let this narrative to be mistaken in any way possible even after my demise. That is part of my identity and destiny.

Never Was Born to Carry Your Damn Lies

I was never brought into this universe to carry your lies and cross. Don't let your mind be confused by those damn lies. I am neither an Arab nor a European nor a sellout. I am the Negus. Thus, carry your own damn lies and cross. Don't try to convert me! I've been there, done that!

Don't you cherish democracy of ideas and liberty?

Why do you want me dead for speaking my mind?

Heaven! Are you a witness to all this madness?

Or should I call hell as a witness as well and expect hell to tell the truth?

Fuck out here! Spiritually speaking, at peace I am, and I see beyond death.

Rejected

There must be confusion in heaven.

Rejected in heaven, I am. Should I knock on the door of hell?

Of course not! Not worth the pain and suffering. I have an undeclared third option.

Living in a Racist Country

Living in a racist country, you will learn a lot about humanity.

Live in a racist universe, you will learn a lot about your own emotions, dilemma, history, forged history, a lot about evil, hell, and your mind will never cease to question both masters: God and the devil.

Why do we exist? Why did God choose us, not any other kind? Then you may end up becoming an atheist. Well, this is a possibility just a possibility.

Life and death are challenges we cannot escape, only accept as factual matters of divinity, maybe not for some. Life and death are not illusions because they are here to stay, no matter what your illusions are.

Never Seek Guidance from Hell

Even in my most trouble phases of life including internal and external spiritual questioning, I never seek guidance from hell, never. God is my witness in case you don't believe me.

The Battle of the Souls

The battle of the souls has begun; theirs must burn in hell while ours shall live in heaven for eternity.

I Don't Live for the Moments

I don't live for the moments. I live for the ages, the ages to come.

I See the Greatness

I see the greatness of God in nature; thus, I don't need heaven to convince me nor a building called church, mosque, temple, the temple of falsehood, the temple of truth, whatever else is out there. Nature is factual enough as far as I am concerned.

You Are in God's Hands

No worries! You are in God's hands. Nothing harmful will happen to you. You are always going to be because you are meant to be by God's divinity.

Don't Kill Creativity

Don't kill creativity by censorship and fear of the unknown and known. This is addressed to religion and government. We don't need government and religion to remind us of morality. We know with certainty what morality is. Let us intrigue and stimulate minds for the betterment of humanity.

Is It Better?

Is it better to think or not to?

In a corrupt society it can be a curse or a blessing, a blessing that can lead to enlightenment or a curse that may lead to death.

Power without Consideration

Power without consideration for all citizens is a recipe for injustice, riot, and disaster just by simple logic. Those who seek power without consideration for all citizens must never have it because they will abuse it with certainty. All must be considered without exception including the crooks' fate with the spirit of the law as it was meant to be.

Turn Out to Be

They are going to turn out to be who they are going to turn out to be because of the environment and past history. Not surprising, just logical.

Competing against the Dead

Are you competing against the dead?

Why?

Why not just be appreciative?

Or are you showing your appreciation by competing against the dead?

Folly!

Luck

Luck is defined and conceived in heaven but forged in hell. No wonder, hell will always be the place it was meant to be hell.

Please Lift My Spirit

Please lift my spirit with divinity and divinity only. I beg not to ask twice.

Since

Since the first time we showed up in this universe, the stakes and challenges have never ceased nor stopped to evolve. The spirits of our ancestors live and carry on. We are the reflection of greatness and divinity; never forget even if told otherwise.

Human Spirit

The human spirit is a source of divinity that sometimes commits evil unfortunately. We know this by experience.

Censorship

Whatever you are censoring is still floating in our minds anyway. What a waste!

The Memo

Did you get the memo?
    No, I did not.
    Well, you will get it in hell.
    Well, I will never get it because I will be chilling in heaven with God literally.

Penned

Not penned yet, but it will be.

The Dilemma

My wrongs are only written in hell, and my rights are in heaven. If you would like to deal with my wrongs, you will have to deal with the master of hell. Just be prepared as a matter of caution.

I Have Not Spoken Yet

I have not spoken yet, nor am I in full gear mode, and hell is trembling of fear. The master of hell is hiding.

How Much...?

How much did the master of hell buy your soul for?

I can match this to liberate your soul. You have the audacity to kill and sell mankind literally then forge history, blame others for your own ills. Do you want redemption lost soul?

They Can Ignore Me

They can ignore me on earth meanwhile I am not being ignored in heaven and hell.

The Question Is Simple

The question is simple.

Why do you have so much contempt for the truth?

When will your demagoguery cease?

Why do you despise to death, Negus?
Aren't you a racist?
Don't you love justice and liberty?
Will you kill for money?
Will you sell your soul for money?
Will you sell humans for money literally?

Zone of Creativity

I am living in a zone of creativity that cannot be undone, destiny at its very best as someone might say.

Groomed

I was groomed in heaven to lead radical change on earth. Please follow me and have faith. God is always with us.

Pity

I can always find pity in my heart for myself and others whenever need be. Therefore, I don't need yours.

Terrified

Terrified that knowledge will possibly lead to my demise I decided to become ignorant.

I Welcome Knowledge

Terrified that ignorance may possibly lead to my demise, I welcome knowledge.

What Is This Madness?

What is this madness?

Shall we just sit and watch while being killed in silence?

Our anger must resonate on earth, hell, and heaven.

If earth, hell, and heaven shall tremble altogether, so let it be.

Fuck this madness!

Dare to test us; here is your result.

The Cause Is Righteous

The cause is righteous; therefore, we will fight for it, and hell will fight back. At our finest we will be. At our finest we will win because we are righteous and always have been.

They Robbed Us

They robbed us of everything, and I mean everything literally, even our birthright to protest against injustice, to protect ourselves, and what else do I know. Hell yeah! They must be sent to hell unquestionably. Do you hear me, God? Can you hear us, God?

Just Overwhelming Sadness

My emotions are characterized by overwhelming sadness. How do you go from a Negus to being a sellout Negro for the racists, for the irresponsible white power structure? Do you feel this much of self-pity with respect to your skin? Does your mind live in hell? What happened? Please help me understand your psyche in your own word. Can you? In all honesty without being a con artist.

Still Prisoner

They are still prisoner of mastered lies. Therefore, I intend to set them free by stating only factual facts, still prisoner of lies until liberated.

Free or Not

Only if my death will free them, as a result, let them be free if not well let them remain prisoners.

Tragedy

She seems to be followed by tragedies. Is this destiny or tragedy from the script?

They Tried to Bury Me

They despised me and killed me with hate. Surprisingly they are trying to bury me with love and tears. The contradictions are mesmerizing; may hell fall inside their souls for eternity; no forgiveness is allowed in this case.

Only misery shall follow them. Damned for eternity they are, I command.

Not Biased

Not biased, just a concerned citizen.

Not Concerned

Not concerned, just a biased citizen.

Being Challenged

I am being challenged by society, and I am challenging society back, and neither of us is enjoying these moments. Well, maybe later we will as we get wiser and mature. Thus, only time will tell.

Simplicity

I desire my joy and moments of uniqueness to be captured in simplicity, not complexity.

Born a Sinner

Born a sinner, I shall die a god, a purified god spiritually. However, I shall not be worshiped, just appreciated.

Orders Are Given

Orders are given to be disregarded and dismissed here; this is not the army or religion.

No Code of Honor

She did a brilliant job by poisoning those valuable memories with lies; therefore, they have become worthless and insignificant. She has no code of honor; may her dishonesty be celebrated to unknown places. What a pity!

Wake Up, Dear

Wake up, dear! The dream is over. Whatever power you dreamed you had has been negated with reality. Now watch reality and greatness unfold to your dislike.

God's Church

God's church, God's rules and dogma.

"Since this is my church, my rules and dogma are applied," says the impostor.

See you in hell, I say, son of darkness, a con artist.

Many Things

There are many things I can prove to you, but there is none I want to prove to you due to your own code of dishonesty and insanity.

Please Rise above Pity

Please, I beg you to rise above pity for the sake of sanity.

No need to fret. I am going to for the betterment of humanity.

What Is Life Worth?

What is life worth?

Life is worth nothing without at least one conviction to lean on.

How Can You Defend This?

How can you defend this?

I can because I am insanely still smart. This is not heaven. Next question, please.

Reservoir of Anger

I have a reservoir of anger to let go.

Do you want to be the beneficiary?

The Candidates

Should I upset the people who are buying me to buy voters' votes?

Or should I upset the voters?

Quite a dilemma, I must confess.

Damn, democracy!

Vive, tyranny!

Process

Process the truth please.
    Sorry, I can't.
    Please process the lies.
    Of course, I am glad to.

They Call to Boycott My Ideas

They call for the boycott of my ideas based solely on their disagreement not merit. I call for tyranny so my ideas can be forcefully imposed on their damn minds of intolerance. Welcome to a new democracy called tyranny. Or welcome to a new tyranny called democracy. Politicking loves to trick your mind. This newfound entertainment must be fun and funny for the ages.

I Am Not Here to Inform

I am not here to inform, rather to be informed of the transgressions that exist between mankind.

History Made

History is made and forged to please certain minds, certain minds only. How convenient?

Looking for Answers

While they are looking for answers, I am looking for questions.

Can't we just compliment each other?

Ancestry

I come from the line of warriors and legends seen and unseen. Thus, how can I betray them and become a coward, a sellout? Impossible is the answer.

The Judiciary

The judiciary shall be independent or this democracy is doomed to tyranny. Enjoy tyranny, fellas, whenever the time comes, hopefully later than sooner. I will be chilling in heaven by that time. Sorry to leave you with tears and exhaustion. Well, I am extremely confident that you will be able to find your way to heaven or hell.

What Do You Want?

What do you want?

Do you want the law of the land? Or do you want the law of heaven to apply to your existence?

The truth shall not be revealed to you that the existence of heaven is only imaginary.

I Don't Mean to Complain

I don't mean to complain for my lack of understanding. I am complaining for an unfit and incompetent educational system, which leads to my lack of understanding often.

Great Minds

Great minds have always walked in divinity, then the earth, and I am no exception to the rule of nature, the rule of divinity.

Climbing Mountains

We will climb these mountains of insanity by defiance without approval of any kind from anybody including God and the master of darkness if so wished. Fuck this madness to its core!

Quarrel

No worries, their quarrel will end in heaven and hell, not on earth.

Emotions

Without emotions, there are neither art nor science of any kind, thus no progress. This goes back to the Negus origin of mankind.

The Gift

The gift was never sought but given by divinity.

Surrounded

Surrounded by mediocrity, mediocrity awaits.
   Surrounded by greatness, greatness awaits.

For Every Single Question

For every single question you may have including their variability, the final answer is invariable and will always be. I don't live for the moments. I live for the ages, the ages to come.

Gold

I will put extremely valuable gold in your hand, and your only duty is to recognize it once awake, but you run the risk of throwing it away if unrecognized.

Darkness Everywhere

There is darkness everywhere you turn, look; and we are not in hell yet, just on earth. Oh! Oh! Sick human mind! Oh!

Oh! Pity! Where is God? You cannot escape the thought, but you can ask, does God exist? The proportion of this darkness seems to indicate the contrary in full light. Please ring the bell of that insanity and fraud—I mean, religion. I can't be condemned for questioning God, can I? What about liberty? What about free will? God knows better than any being.

I Only Offer Two Things

I only offer two things to you for consideration: misery or death. Allow me to clarify or elaborate: If you vote for me, I am going to offer you misery. If not, I offer death by guillotine. This shall be immediate with no possibility of appeal. May tyranny live forever! Damn democracy!

Despite Their Religious Folly

Despite their religious folly, they still are worthy of being saved and sent to hell by the bullet or guillotine if so wish. Never forget I have the last word on this matter.

Bankrupt

Bankrupt they are morally. Therefore, expect hell from them, nothing else. But dream if you want and dream whatever you mind desire; even illusions are included.

I Went to Sleep

I went to sleep in a world of tranquility and woke up in a universe of wars, chaos, pity, countless murders, dried tears from women, dried tears from infants, dried tears from children, dried tears from men, dried tears from the dead, dried tears from our forebears, dried tears to the point of exhaustion, religious folly, and fanatic. Can someone explain? Death is everywhere. The spaces and each living mind are preoccupied by one thought only, deaths. In this precise moment, my soul is ashamed of being part of the human existence and experience. Can we find redemption in human darkness and folly? Born a sinner, I shall die a god so I can transcend this folly, this humanity, and this flesh.

Those Religious Books

If those religious books are fraud and forged, how can you expect sainthood, not folly, murder, and fanatic? Good luck wishing and dreaming of sainthood and heaven while meeting death in the corridor of hell.

Dead Soul

If dealing with a dead and lost soul, fret for your life and soul because you must.

Don't Count on Them

Don't count on them to listen, to reason. Just bullets are going to suffice to send them to hell deservingly so.

Liberty

Liberty speaks they want to murder liberty. Can they? Hell no! Unambiguously they can't is the answer.

Ultimatum

I am given an ultimatum to join either political party. My response is, they are unworthy of any consideration. I am and prefer to stay an independent thinker even in tyranny.

We Are Moving

We are moving from democracy to tyranny because it is best.
May the doors of democracy be closed, never visited again.
If ever visited again, this shall be done in a museum only, the
museum of democracy, and may the doors of tyranny and
hell be opened broadly to the full satisfaction of hell and his
master, maybe her master. I am ignorant if it is *his* or *her*, I
must confess. Does it matter? Hell no! Hell is hell!

The Way It Goes

Pretty stubborn you would say or think.
    Well, I am, and it is a trait of mine.
    If I want you, I have to have you.
    The contrary is true as well.
    That is just the way it goes.

We Will See

The earth was given to them with all things in it to quench
their thirst.
    Will they blow it in chaos, wars, malady of any kind, kill
each other?
    Or will they maintain it with dignity and honor?

Will they teach their progeny love or hate?

What else will the progeny teach themselves?

Time will tell. We will see, don't be surprised because their soul contains enlightenment and evil simultaneously.

What a natural contrast!

Nothing Else

Nothing else comes to mind but pity, only pity for their souls.

Whenever Hell Unleashes Its Wings

Whenever hell unleashes its wings, what will be the course of action to take?

Shall righteousness matter or just evil in the response?

Hell and heaven, darkness and light are diametrically opposed by nature.

Thus, you must choose one, one only.

You Can Claim the Contrary

You can claim the contrary, but nobody wins a war of insanity by insanity, only by sound judgment and reason. That is the challenge. Just ask hell and heaven if in doubt.

They Confirm by Swearing to God

They confirm by swearing to God that they have never read *The Prince* by Niccólo Machiavelli; however, all their evil, trickery, and killing have the unique characteristic and unique touch of Machiavelli. What a strange coincidence indeed!

Simply Called the Infusion

The infusion of new ideas and ideals are unequivocally fundamental to the progress of mankind. Conclusively, it is unfortunate whenever others and many governments use murder and coercion to silent dissidents in the name of law and order, against anarchy, but this is ordered anarchy and corruption anyway. Don't you see the volcano is in the eruption phase? Can't silence me. I'm too divine to be.

The Gate of Hell

The gate of hell should have never been opened; unfortunately, it has been. How do we deal with it is a question of the deepest concern. Shall we pray to God or skip him? That is the question each of us must answer in a thoughtful manner and privately if so deem.

Please Don't Mix Us or Confuse Us

Please don't confuse us; we are not the sons of darkness. To the contrary, we represent enlightenment. Thus, how can we be afraid, afraid of what darkness, afraid of death? Let darkness and death come our way, and they are going to find us standing up firmly and ready to send them into hell in matter of seconds. Never dare to test our will!

This Kind of Evil

This kind of evil is unfathomable unless your mind, spirit, and being live and breathe the oxygen from hell. How can we comprehend this kind of evil? We don't have access to the master of hell as their actions proclaim loudly.

Inhale Love Expel Hate

Inhale the oxygen of love and expel hate from your being. Can mankind exercise this simple act despite all else? Shouldn't I ponder?

All I Need Is to Question

All I need to do is to question that is my solely role and those smart bastards need to come up with solutions or answers. Doesn't my questioning help in the process of finding answers?

If I Shall Die...

If I shall die in the battlefield of hell with respect to my convictions, I will. Never dare to test me, not even the master of hell can.

Just Watch

Just watch. Hate will kill them, and love will save them.

Are they too stupid to distinguish? They keep implementing hate and murder.

To Convince

I am not here to convince nor preach because nobody is worthy of any convincing.

Dare to convince me otherwise.

It's a Man Thing

Simply a man thing, big men do big things and play big games within the natural laws of morality and divinity. Not given to any man.

Behold your Negus!

Tradition

Tradition is invalid here. We implement meritocracy.

Hell with tradition and fraud!

Behold! Natural Cloth!

Wear your natural cloth proudly even while being challenged by insanity and fraud because you are going to be.

Behold your Negus! Behold your Negus as the originator, as the source, as the beginner of humanity, and all else!

The secret of humanity, some mysticisms, certain powers, be it physical, be it spiritual, shall remain within, solely you.

Despite all else, the deepest character of your soul can never be touched by darkness. There is nothing else to comprehend all is mystical.

Divine you are! Behold your Negus!

Grounded

Grounded by humility and grace, I look within and toward the sky in a moment of profound reflection and absolute silence.

Is This a Dream?

Is this a dream? Is this a nightmare? Am I dreaming?

No, it is not. This is reality of distasteful taste, so wake up from your illusion. This is firmly a declaration of intent also called war. We must move courageously. Arm in the air and ready to shoot!

My Trait

By nature, my trait doesn't take very well or kindly any type of menace, be it by mankind, be it by any government, be it by hell, be it by heaven. Finally, the list is complete. Hopefully, you understand and show reverence.

The Plot

Never confuse the plot of a movie, a theatre, and a cinema with reality. Imagination can be just a land of fantasies, unreachable dreams, immoralities, as well as morality. Still learn how best to separate imagination from reality because this process will serve you best in your everyday life.

We Didn't Even Ask

We didn't even ask the apocalyptic offer and these corrupt, insane politicians, these religions still have the audacity to tell us that they will lead us to heaven; not to our surprise they are leading us to hell.

Welcome to hell on earth! Indeed, we are experiencing hell before death. Pity is the only thought crossing my mind nothing else.

Unfortunately They Must Pay

Unfortunately for their liberty they must pay by blood no other type of payment can be accepted. The sooner they understand this, the sooner liberty comes.

Flames

If they cannot reason, as they must, then let darkness come to their doors; let their universe flame with no pity.

I Don't Claim Liberty

I don't claim liberty. I exercise it without permission.

Everybody

Everybody wants to be in charge, even the unqualified ones, and nobody wants to rule on the basis of accountability that democracy demands.

Should we become subjects or slaves of his or her majesty?
Should we welcome tyranny?
Is there anything we can or can't do?
Is there anything we can or can't say?

We Left Them Politicking

We left them politicking for centuries to rule with dignity and honor, but they can't. Never did. Thus, the citizens want that power back peacefully or with guns if they don't cede.

Doubt and Assurance

Where there is doubt, there is at least one question to be asked and answered. Where there is absolute assurance, there is blindness to critical thinking. Needless to say, the consequences can be deadly.

The Mockery of Sane and Sound Intellectualism

Ideas, ideals, facts, opinions are all violated by the lack of consistency, by the lack of a clear understanding of the nature of the problem including its origins, expansions, and precise consequences. This is simply a mockery of sane and sound intellectualism. Also defined as the anarchy of the intellect or the intellectualism of anarchy, coined by Mbuta Luyinduladio Celly. The anarchy of the intellect is always followed by anarchy. How surprising. A fitting example of immeasurable proportions and folly is the second invasion of Iraq in March 20, 2003.

Now! Take a critical look at your anarchy, hell, and the anarchy of the intellect if and only if you possess the critical mental capacity otherwise just observe.

Shamelessly, the argument continues in full support of
the anarchy of the intellect so anarchy can extend its reaches.
  Folly! And only folly!
  Who damned these beings?
  Is God the author? Is darkness the author?
  Sadly intriguing, discontent I am.

No Status

I am not preoccupied by status.
  Others, well, may be.
  Why should I be?
  I am the status.
  I am the Negus!

Discontent

They claim their discontent on all matters and always
are; discontent they can stay. My reach and power are
uncontested. Thus, I just mock their discontent in silence.
Damned they can be! I am also discontent with their
irrational discontent.

The Beauty of Life

The undeniable beauty of life is simplistic because it resides in free will.

Not a Laughing Matter!

This is not a laughing matter, I must emphasize, and this was never meant to be either.

Thus, can we conclude that it became a laughing matter by accident? What an irony? What an emblematic conclusion!

You can conclude as you see fit. I am just stating the intent at the origin.

Did They Claim…?

Did they claim the baton of intellectualism for themselves only?

Didn't they claim the baton of ignorance and savageness for us by all means, did they?

Since facts, ideas, opinions, and ideals all prove the contrary, we can conclude that they are indeed the representation of the intellectualism of anarchy also defined as the mockery of sane and sound intellectualism. Not surprised at all because biases are deeply seeded in their souls and spirits.

Darkness be praised as they always say in obscurity.

Trying to Define

They are trying to define what they can't.

They are trying to comprehend what they can't. Nonetheless, they will, in both cases and many others to come, use the concept of the anarchy of the intellect or the intellectualism of anarchy. As assumed correctly, the fallout will be anarchy.

Only Reality

Only reality is facing them with courage, and they can't face reality with courage. How telling?

Extremely Sad!

Before calamity and disaster strike, they cannot think properly. After disaster and calamity struck, they still cannot reason accordingly. Extremely sad!

I Am Not God

I am not God, rather the master of hell, and this shall be obvious to the angels, but it is not surprisingly so. I am walking in heaven without boundary of any kind to my surprise. Even the devil can surprise himself.

Well, what a nightmare in heaven!

Don't Paraphrase Me

Please don't dare to paraphrase me!

Quote me! I am clear and eloquent enough!

Never Cease to Hope

Never cease to hope the answer is simple I am simply optimistic by nature despite darkness. Light will always conquer darkness no matter what. It is simply a matter of time.

History

History doesn't seem to teach them anything valuable. How sad. Ironically, they are the owners, makers of that history. I insist they are the architects of that history. This point must be driven home with clarity and passion.

Losing the Ability to Fear

In case you lose the ability to fear, you lose your humanity. May God grant us courage and the ability to love.

What Is Your Religion?

What is your religion, sir?

I have none. I am a divine man. I am divinity itself. I am the Negus!

Behold Negus!

Whenever Realities and Facts...

Whenever realities and many facts travel in front of me, I suddenly become blind even though I am not. Difficult to explain, I must confess. Am I being tricked? Can't figure this out sadly!

They've Got the Nerves of Hell

They've got the nerves of hell to dare to discriminate and enslave us, then have the audacity to forge all things to their satisfaction.

Who are those people?
How come you do not know them?
Are you stating that this forgery is working?
Do you really want to know who they are?
Hell yeah!
Well! Those fuckers!
Can you see them now?
Confused, he is. No wonder!

Are You Absorbing All This Garbage?

Are you absorbing all this garbage as they expect you to?
Of course!
Well, don't become an imbecile. Stay smart and critical. However, play the fool to satisfy their foolishness.

The Absence of Logic

In the absence of logic, death by coercion is the king, and cowardliness is the queen.

What is your preference, king or queen?

If I Shall Die

If I shall die, I shall die for the cause of righteousness and ideals, not the contrary, so my soul can never be ridiculed in pity, so my soul can never be ridiculed in the land of darkness.

Do you expect them to understand?

Of course not! Since when did enlightenment and darkness change seats?

Radical

I don't claim to have received the call from heaven or hell to bring religion, misery, darkness, or insanity on this universe. I am a simple man with a simple life who wants the simple joy of life. Can I be left alone peacefully?

Unconventional

These follies demand an unconventional tone, character, an extraordinary intelligence, and I will provide these. Others can still be conventional and ordinary. What is liberty worth without the will to exercise it despite the treat?

Never dare to touch me, and never dare to abuse me.

Field of Study

On his field of study, he is extremely gifted, we must confess. However, outside the field of his study, he is simply an average man who leans close and closer to imbecility and stupidity in terms of knowledge; surprisingly true is the case. How is this possible?

Citizenship

Let me pause for a second. I don't think that any state has a right to take away citizenship of its citizens in any circumstances, heinous criminals or not. While the state has a right to praise its heroes loudly, the state has a right to access legal means to condemn to death or life in prison without the possibility of parole. Once again, the ideas and means to strip away citizenship by legal means shall never be granted despite the grandeur of the crime; just apply justice within the framework of reason, not fear and insanity. How would you justify stateless citizens? Isn't this the abuse of power? Used to power, they abuse it for entertainment, their own.

The Courage of Opinion

Can you have the courage of your opinion?

Of course! I always do as a matter of fact if you can just dare to check me.

Keep in Check

The state must be kept in check because the state is always involved in the business of criminality and order, a balancing act of sanity and insanity. Intriguing dichotomy! Teach us morality then, damn it! No wonder we live in a universe of trauma and dramatic events.

Unsaid

Best unsaid than said. Silence is gold in this matter because stupidity and treachery will always prevail somehow, no matter what, no matter the cause, and no matter the argument.

The Same Thing

We are looking at the same thing with different emotions, ideas, ideals, opinions, and the only major difference is, I have access to keys and they don't, and they are quick to critique, only critique.

The Option

I will tell you what is in my heart, not head. Or would you rather hear what is my head instead of heart. You can never hear both.

No Need to Fret

No need to fret. I will enter the corridor of hell with mystics, mysteries, and extraordinaries even the master of hell will never dare to touch me.

Not Too Many Sides

There are not too many sides to this story. Just two: wrong versus righteousness. And I stand on the side of righteousness. Pick up your side in daylight for all to see!

Never Compromise

Compromise with the devil; next he will demand your soul, so never compromise.

I Don't Hate Your Manners

I don't hate your manners. Why should I? I pity your education.

Always

I have always walked the earth as the Negus, not a slave.

Go back and check! Why should I start now?

Why would you enslave me? Folly!

Why don't you enslave yourself and enjoy many benefits of miseries?

Damned and doomed you shall be by darkness. Otherwise, how can this be explained?

What a Contrast!

The racists are looking at me with nothing else except racist emotions, death threats, and I am looking at them with humanity even though their souls are lost in darkness. Where should I go for help, to heaven or hell? Where the folly is incomprehensible those damned racists are religious.

Do you mean kind of?

Yeah! I mean sort of.

The Code of Silence

Finally, they came out of their sleep and decided to call the demagogue a monster, a cancer to be cured of. However, they are complicit in building the monster, in developing the cancer instead of curing it.

The code for corruption is silence, manipulation, power by any means, and the one for enlightenment is defiance and eruption. We don't take orders of silence whether it is a democracy or a dictatorship. What else do you have in mind? Fuck this folly!

Ruled

Ruled by robbers, criminals, crooks, the men and women of many adjectives and nouns. What kind of language would they understand, death and guns? This life is intriguing. Can heaven call my number? Is it hell instead?

Never Drop the Torch

We never drop the torch of courage and history; we carry it with great pride.

This is a new generation of Negus!

A New System

Democracy has a tendency of being corrupted, dictatorship is unworthy of our code of honor, and communism is dismissed without consideration because this political system is not worth it; that is their opinion. What else should we implement? Maybe we just need the deepest reform possible.

Well, what about tyranny?

Well, allow us to consider it in darkness first. Then we will bring it to light if deemed necessary.

Crossed the Line

They concluded that I crossed the line of morality. In case I did, I claim ignorance. What is morality? It is a matter of opinion, conviction, and cultural adequacy and inadequacy. Can we at least agree that I haven't crossed the line of freethinking? And you have to be a freethinker to understand this.

Savageness

Savageness is learned not embedded in blood by birthright.

The Ruler

The ruler wants to impose hell on all except the establishment. Will the people resist by revolutionary measures? Or will they give in? Berserk the ruler is. Berserk he shall die someone says.

Radicalism

Radicalism is what sustains the soul of mankind in terms of innovations, pushing forbidden boundaries, fighting evil, and looking at enlightenment with glory and awe. Henceforth, call me a radical if so wished. I was meant to be.

The Shadow

Can I see to whom I am talking to?
   Nope! You can't?

Why not?

I am the shadow. I can be heard not seen. I am here to punish evil and save the righteous.

No Moral Obligation

I am not interested in morality, nor do I have any moral obligation to any. I am the master who reigns in darkness for eternity. Any question? Please direct questions to God because I don't intend to answer any.

Where Is the Plan?

Where is the plan?

There is none. We are moving with the flow and improvisation.

Things of Dream

These are things of dream, but you will see them in reality because time has come.

Reversed Paradise Theory

On earth, the trustworthiness shall die and the crook must survive, be glorified. This is known in hell as the reversed paradise theory. What a universe of pity!

Never Meant to Be

This was never meant to be, and I find strength, comfort, and peace of mind looking at reality, not wishful thinking.

It Was a Brilliant Idea

It was a brilliant idea that ended in the garbage of history because there was no implementation, no follow up, no one to understand.

Don't Pretend Ignorance

Surrounded by immorality, I will act in accordance. Don't pretend ignorance.

I Lied to God

I lied to God, and he did not know. I find the thought intriguing somehow. I'll ask for forgiveness later, maybe not.

A Grand Theater

The universe is nothing else but a grand theater for morality and immorality experiences wherever you dare to look.

I Don't Sleep…

I don't sleep on their worries. I sleep looking at the future including the mystic.

In the Land

In the land of berserk, entertainment always comes free.

Any Argument in a Democracy

Any argument in a democracy, as faulty as it may sound, is best as long as people are awoken. What is the essence of a democracy? I dare to ask. May this question carry your mind and emotion to a place of enlightenment and tolerance not darkness and death.

Giving a Meaning

Giving a meaning to a senseless and meaningless life can be tragic in so many ways.

Paint the Façade

Paint the façade, and that should be enough of trickery.
    Nope! It won't work.
    I guarantee it will, rest assured.
    Paint the façade, and we shall see.

They Want Blood

They want blood. We will give them their own and send them to hell.

Demystified

I have never demystified their claimed superiority because they did by ignorance, folly, and forgery. How clever. The throne has always been a façade just dare to check and reason.

Worth Noting

A simple thought that says it all in Lingala: "Tambola na mokili omona makambo." (Just walk or travel in this universe in order to see things that will puzzle your mind, things that are going to leave your emotions unsettled, things of a different nature.) Nowadays all you really need to do is log in the Internet to be puzzled. Time has changed! Time has changed! What else can I say? Mankind has come a long way still there is a long way forward.

Whatever Is Convenient and Comfortable

Should I do whatever is convenient and comfortable for their minds?

Of course not! I don't intend to because there are too many challenges to address. Each soul can define its own entitlement, convenience, inconvenience, what is comfortable or not, and proceed accordingly.

The World

You don't have the world you wish for rather you have the one you are born into with its greatness, pain, pity, and miseries. What will your role be, amplify the pain, pity, and miseries?

How Would You Like to Rewrite These Wrongs?

How would you like to rewrite these wrongs by poetry or by the language of death spoken only by guns and fire?

Well, my intent is to rewrite these wrongs by using both methods because poetry only is insufficient at best.

The Same Old Trick the Same Result

After voting overwhelmingly for the politician and gaining power, not only does he think but he acts as if we owe him a birthday cake, dinner, dessert, soup, and lunch. No matter the order, we must pay, or he will make us pay for our vote, our mistake, our critique, what he calls our stupidity. What a mask! Damn! Shall we pray to God or to evil? Oh! Oh! I almost forgot about the tip also known as gratuity we owe him that too. How dare I forget? Damn me! Silly me! Folly! The mystic ought to be called into this matter. Please come and save us of this absurdity and great folly.

Uniquely Masterful

Uniquely masterful not by birthright rather by fate, I am.
Can't you see?
Should I remind you?
Well, you have been then.

Paying Homage

If the credentials of hip-hop started in the street of the Bronx in New York at 1520 Sedgwick Avenue on Saturday, August 11, 1973, by Clive Campbell also known as DJ Kool Herc followed in the footstep by Kevin Donovan also known as Afrika Bambaataa, Joseph Saddler also known as Grandmaster Flash, and Melvin Glover also known as Grandmaster Melle Mel, it must be emphasized that this is no longer a matter of many opinions but factual. Henceforth, no matter the evolution, Hip-hop's truest credentials will always remain street-based because its soul is at the origin where the revolution of this art form originated from the brouhaha of a corrupt universe. These pioneers shall never be buried in the list of the forgotten because collectively they have given the universe the positive vibes. History has a tendency of forgetting or being corrupted at its core. We could sit back and ponder endlessly. This task is easiest than navigating the galaxies in order to create something of extraordinary measure, nature, and universally acclaimed critically. Reverence shall be shown where it ought to be. The deepest gratitude is expressed.

Negus, at their very best, created and revolutionized many civilizations and cultures throughout history for the rest to claim and consume. Still the disdain continues. Thus, both confusion and lies sit and have the audacity to question the truest author with a straight face. Doesn't happen only in theater and cinema. I understand to some degree the culture including the frustration as part of the narrative to say and mean we had enough of this bullshit. Fuck you! Vulgarity is just the reflective mirror of the pain and society we are supposed to thrive in, further from the truth. Absolutism in any matter is just a matter of dreams even whenever the truth is absolute.

Finally, all can hear multiple voices screaming, not knowing where they are coming from including their authors are unknown as well: "Flip the script again and again until we get this right. We have done this before, not once, haven't we? Why is this taking too long? Nobody can stop us. Aren't we the damned masters? This Black gold belongs to us, only us. Rewrite that damn script." Then the voices are vanishing one by one progressively in darkness. Obscure meetings are taking place in darkness. Simultaneously, something mystical is happening in the abstract. Of course, this must be felt not seen.

Hip-hop brilliance and creativity with its flaws are here to stay whether recognized or not, whether disliked or not. As a matter of fact, does this matter? The question begs itself to be asked only not answered.

Who has the last word?

This is a new generation of Negus! Put them up! Keep them up! Damn fists in the air, Negus!

Cut the Check

Cut the check!

How come? What do you mean? Aren't you a slave, and I am the master?

Nope! Not anymore. I just freed myself. Do you have a problem with that? Look here! Do you see what I can see?

Yes, sir! I do, and here is your check.

Absolutism

Absolutism in any matter always worries me. I prefer a certain reflection of open dissent.

There Is No Third Option

There are both men and women who refuse categorically to come to terms with who they are naturally, therefore, refusing to assume their manhood and womanhood respectively. Ironically, there is no third option. Will nature test their imagination? Will they defy nature to what extent?

No Significance, Just Ignore

If there is no significance, why give it a meaning? Let it stay irrelevant.

I Have Seen the Universe

I have seen the universe through the eyes of God. Then I have also seen it through the eyes of darkness. What is there to conclude? I don't know.

Intriguing Silence

Whatever you are not stating with your silence is intriguing to all.

Please I would like to understand the statement and meaning of your intriguing silence.

Are you saying, "Fuck them," with an intriguing silence? After all, this is a free country, so no worries. You indeed can speak your mind. However, silence is part of the fabric of liberty.

I disagree it is not. Therefore, he must speak. If he does not, I am not afraid to use torture or enhanced techniques as some have the audacity to blur it.

Don't you know that silence leads to dictatorship, communism, or fascism? Speak, he must. Fuck him! I am returning the favor, that's all.

I Dare Not Question

I dare not question things I cannot see nor comprehend. Why should I open my mind to torture with consent? I let others enjoy themselves.

Should I...?

Should I swing my religious sword to convert the infidel? Or should I pray to God to convert them? May be I should just swing the sword because it is less confusing and more convincing. Some will conclude folly; I conclude God's will. God is mystical; thus, I can claim the mystic. Darkness is somewhere in my soul talking to me. Should I ignore or not?

Where Is the Maestro?

Where is the maestro?

Here I am!

Well, you can't be. This is ridiculous to say the least. This cannot be!

If you are, where is the orchestra?

Well, I am the maestro without the orchestra. The maestro of maestri, I am without the orchestra.

Well, we have never seen anything like this.

Well, if you say so, dear, you never supposed to have had until this precise moment. Not to insist, but without the orchestra, I am the maestro of maestri.

Did You Learn Anything?

Did you learn anything?

Of course not!

What do you mean by "Of course not"?

Didn't she or he teach?

Of course both of them did. Nothing of significance was learnt because nothing of significance was taught, just noise followed by the brouhaha. My mind is still empty and thirsty for knowledge.

Interesting!

Interesting it is, depending on your angle of view.

The Maestro Always Conducts

I don't need to step into the microphone to burn these lines, to speak to the deity, to the ancestors, and God. I am the mirror. The maestro of maestri always conducts; even in darkness, he brings light and enlightenment.

He Is Uncommon

He is uncommon to most men—a kind of enigma because he is interested in knowledge and solitude; meanwhile the most are interested in ephemera, which in turn make them ordinary.

The Bar

Raise the bar! Raise the threshold! They refuse to in a categorical manner. However, willingly they decide to lower it to the point of imbecility. Who is to say they can't? What is liberty without the ability to exercise it? Worthless!

Simply Amused

Simply amused, not shocked. Certain minds are pondering how I am not. My mind did ponder and came to its own conclusion, which is amusement only. Therefore, shocked you should not be.

These Are Words

These are words of a con artist, words of treachery, words that carry no weight, no truth whatsoever. Therefore, simply disregard them. Or accept them to your own peril. Should I wish you any luck? Do you need any?

The Star

What kind of star is it?

It's a mystical one because it shines, moves only within including in the hidden galaxies. Thus, don't look for it or try to comprehend because lost you will be. There is nothing to comprehend.

I Simply Don't...

I simply don't emulate them; instead, they emulate me.

Am I not the Negus? Am I? Isn't this a known fact?

Is it? Damn it! Double-check history and the source for certainty!

Treachery and forgery be damned!

Behold your Negus!

Are You Trying Tyranny on Me?

Are you trying tyranny on me?

Of coursc! No worries, this is just an experiment before I implement this on the general population. Yeah! Those fools. My subjects. Says the unidentified, ambitious man and future king with no royal progeny.

The Court Orders

The court orders, and we disobey because the court is corrupted and incompetent to handle any matter of great importance or not. Therefore, lost a little bit of legitimacy, it had. In turn, we the people order the court and its illegitimate government to dissolve and disband peacefully effective immediately or face war, death, and hell. We intend to implement the French Revolution of 1789 once again. The difference is no corrupt fucking Napoleon Bonaparte will emerge to confiscate power. Bring his damned soul back! Bring the doomed impostor back so he can be passed on to the guillotine, only after due process for betraying the revolution ideals and principles. Of course! We can guarantee his wicked ass that. Doesn't he still like champagne? My assumption is he does. And if this assumption is proven to be correct, then he shall enjoy the guillotine as well. Isn't the guillotine French just like champagne? Bring his wicked ass back to the court for his deeds, misdemeanors, felonies, follies, treasons—in one word, crimes committed against mankind and fellow citizens. The same is true for fucking Leopold II, and these are Europeans among great men, great treacheries, great fraud, great impostors, great heroes, greatest crooks, grotesque criminals, greatest murderers, greatest looters, greatest thieves, and the list goes on.

Somehow, someway the king and the emperor both have always been naked still held in the highest regard possible. Thus, the throne has always been a farce and a fraud. Don't you remember the Congo Free State? Even the greatest irony is in the name. Given by whom you should ask? Is your memory lagging? Or are you just ignorant to the point of imbecility and stupidity? You are not suffering from aphasia, are you?

These are the men we must praise and kneel to.

These are the follies our minds and spirits must deal with and confront if we deem to stay sane and rational. Please consider this as a process of enlightenment, the cure of lies, the medicine of sanity. Don't you want to be cured of lies, do you?

These are the masters of unimaginable criminalities who are always looked in light, enlightenment, not darkness and the spirit of evil.

Welcome to the earth! The land of follies and many deaths, in many forms, natural and unnatural!

How dare he? Would they say or question with audacity?

How dare I not? I am pondering, and I always ponder with my own audacity and courage. Who gives you the right to fuck all else beyond the limit of extremity and reason? God? Darkness? Evil?

Then bring death to those who dare to speak up, challenge your insanity, and question your actions of destruction, drama, and trauma.

Folly! Fuck it! Teach me democracy and liberty then!

Don't you know that in the cycle of birth, a renegade is always born identified only by the mystic?

This is not fucking France after all with its own multiple contradictions bearing the flag of the universal declaration of human rights and guns simultaneously to suppress and deny those same rights to others.

Fucking hypocrite! Look no further than the land of the birth of humanity. With an extraordinary audacity, without guilt, without confession, they dare say that all must be forgotten, but they did not even confess their multiple sins. Moreover, they have a tendency of forgetting that this is not the corrupt church. The teachers of universal morality we beg to be taught morality.

Did you get the sarcasm?

Sorry, I did not.

You are too smart, huh?

Did you get the new one? Huh!

Please rewind both! Lost he looks and must be.

The absurdity of existence is not only seen in theater and cinema.

All the dead and living are pondering. Where is our due process? The continent shall simply withdraw from that façade that theater that fraud called the international court of justice (injustice) that judges and condemns them like stolen properties.

Fuck the court! Can you hear me? Got it? Since when did you become deaf? Always pretend to be deaf and blind in most matters of rationality anyway, not surprising.

Don't you know who you truly are?

How can you be so lost to the point of desperation?

Don't you remember anything else?

Don't you remember Timbuktu's greatness as an example?

Don't you remember Timbuktu as the center of knowledge of the universe?

The diversity of manuscripts is still there as of today as facts.

Don't you remember the Kongo Kingdom in its glory?

What happened?

Too divine to be silenced you are!

Negus, wake up! You are the Negus, aren't you? The birth, the end of humanity and all else!

Born a sinner, living among sinners, I shall transcend this humanity, this folly, and this flesh so I can die a god simply meant to be this way by fate and mysticism.

How Does Liberty...?

How does liberty fair with the truth?

Well, they dislike it to great length with certainty whenever coming from Negus.

Absurdity of existence! Not true!

I concur!

Actually, I concur with him or her.

Yes! Truth is spoken!

I Must Send Shock Waves

I must send shock waves to their minds.

I must send shock waves to their spirits.

I must send shock waves to the spirit of darkness and hell.

I must send shock waves to God and heaven.

I must send shock waves to the universe.

I must send shock waves to the mystic.

I must send positive shock waves and vibes to the lineage and the very first Negus who has ever walked in this universe. Reverence is expressed!

Here I am. Can you feel me by the spirit?

Here I travel. Can you see me in the galaxies?

Uniquely masterful, I move and flow like any other maestri.

Now! Dare to claim your intellectual superiority again on Negus! Still fools will!

There Are Things

There are things you will never know.

There are things I will never explain.

There are things you will never comprehend.

There are things best kept in absolute silence.

There are things best kept in their absolute mystical nature.

Certain things are just meant to be because they simply are and must be accepted as such.

Conquered, I Am

Conquered by your spirit, I am. Then, unable to resist your beauty, as a result, your silhouette conquers me as well. Therefore, it must be concluded that I am a prisoner by will and fate, so I refuse to be released. The only matter is I want to savor your love. Can I? Am I late? Destiny! Never dare to set me free!

The Black Ink

If you ever decide or dare to touch the pen, then touch it with courage and a unique swagger. I mean, let the black ink speak.

Stay In Your Lane!

Have some code of conduct!
　Have some code of honor!
　Have some class!
　Have some manners!
　Of course you have rights, you always will.
　Still don't be a bitch, don't become a bitch, and bitch about it.
　If this is your only desire, then you will be treated as such.
　Can you stay in your lane?
　I am not one of those lunatic religious fanatics.
　Have some decency!
　Staying on your lane or not, it does not matter to me. I mean exercise your liberty as wished and pay for the consequences.
　Fair enough! I must say.
　I know my lane always do.

Life

Life is a perpetual journey of trilogy in a pondering sense between: God, evil, and death.

Why Should I?

Why should I choose between irrationality and folly? As if my spirit is a prisoner of both.

The Black Way

How do you want to proceed or do this?

The Black way!

What do you mean?

I mean this must be done the Black way, unapologetically and with excellence. Disregard the noise!

Moral Truths

Why would you waste your time in pursuit of moral truths?

There is none. This is the Earth, not heaven. Are you confused? The question is why?

Ask God if still in doubt. I hope he answers. In case he does not, knock on hell's doors.

A Piece of Art

They will either love it or despise it, and that is how a piece of art is always viewed—rightfully so because taste is a matter of preference and liberty. Therefore, don't become a piece of art meaning difficult to fathom, difficult to deal with, difficult to analyze and comprehend. At the end, you are just a human being, maybe artfully designed, by whom is another matter of disagreement.

We Want to Be

We want to be but can't be. Therefore, we remain unwillingly the property or properties of the wicked master or masters.

Can we just be, can't we?

Some want to be others don't.

What a dilemma!

She Is a Capitalist Entrepreneur

How did the conversation go?

I really don't know what to say. I really don't know how best to phrase this.

I don't get it! Can you elaborate further?

If you cannot understand, no further explanation is deemed necessary. Here is the explanation. She is a capitalist, a capitalist entrepreneur at the core. She is selling what was meant to be free by consent, the natural thing. Daringly, she solicits even whenever unwanted.

How come? I thought she was a goddess. Isn't she?

The question does not deserve to be answered in light of my explanation.

It's business.

Yeah! It's business, angel!

Soul Searching

The question keeps coming.

Don't you have any soul searching to do?

I said, "Nope! I am cool like God himself. Does God have any soul searching to do? What about the devil? Shouldn't we start with them first? Should we?"

To mock this absurdity of existence as far as I am concerned, I intend to perform my soul searching after my demise, not before.

How can you not enjoy this absurdity of existence while we exist? Why would I dare question my soul? Absurdity of absurdities! Folly of follies! Theater of theaters! Grandest theater of all! I am content like God and discontent like the spirit of obscurantism. You can't be sorry! If you can, let your mind picture that!

Show Me

Please show me a government without tyranny tendencies, blood in its affairs be it its own citizens or foreigners, and I will show you God and the devil simultaneously sitting at the same throne and conversing in secret.

The Last Touch of Genius

Oh! Oh! Shots are fired!

Be cool and don't be confused, fool! Shots are not fired. Instead shock waves are sent to heaven and hell, to God and evil, to the mystic, to the ancestors, to the galaxies, and on earth.

The end is near. Can you feel it? Can you believe this?

Nah! There is no end to this madness, to this folly. Furthermore, there is nothing else to believe in or comprehend.

Well, chapter closes slowly. Book closes meticulously, mystically, and methodically next.

Something mystical appears and disappears in a matter of seconds in an undisclosed location that I cannot discuss further.

The last touch of genius is complete.

MMS IV
NBD

12/29/16

CPSIA information can be obtained
at www.ICGtesting.com
Printed in the USA
FSOW03n0433300816
24342FS